DAILY LIFE IN RENAISSANCE ITALY

THE HORIZON BOOK OF
DAILY LIFE IN RENAISSANCE ITALY

by Charles L. Mee, Jr.

The author dedicates this book

to his daughter, Erin

Published by AMERICAN HERITAGE PUBLISHING CO., INC., New York

Book Trade Distribution by McGRAW-HILL BOOK COMPANY

Library of Congress Cataloging in Publication Data
Mee, Charles L
    The Horizon book of daily life in the Renaissance.
    (Daily life in five great ages of history)
    Bibliography: p. 124
    Includes index.
    1. Florence—Social life and customs.
2. Florence—History—1421-1737. I. Title.
II. Series.
DG735.6.M43   945'.51'05   75-9926
ISBN 0-07-041270-7 (McGraw-Hill)

Contents

CHAPTER I

FLORENCE

"It is undoubtedly a golden age," the humanist Marsilio Ficino wrote five hundred years ago, "which has restored to the light the liberal arts that had almost been destroyed: grammar, poetry, eloquence, painting, sculpture, architecture, music." Ficino's compatriot Leonardo Bruni said of his home town that it "harbors the greatest minds: whatever they undertake, they easily surpass all other men, whether they apply themselves to military or political affairs, to philosophy, or to merchandise." When the architect Leon Battista Alberti came to consider what constituted a perfect human being, he decided he could do no better than to describe himself: "He was devoted," Alberti said of himself, "to the knowledge of the most strange and difficult things. And he embraced with zeal and forethought everything which pertained to fame. He strove so hard to attain a name in modelling and painting . . . his genius was so versatile that you might almost judge all the fine arts to be his. . . . He played ball, hurled the javelin, ran, leaped, wrestled, and above all delighted in the steep ascent of mountains. . . . With his feet together, he could leap over the shoulders of

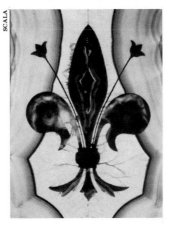

men standing by. . . . With his left foot lifted from the ground to the wall of a church, he could throw an apple into the air so high that it would go far beyond the top of the highest roofs. . . . He despised material gain. . . . He could endure pain, cold and heat, showing by example that men can do anything with themselves if they will."

Succeeding generations have never thought to contradict the appraisal that Renaissance men and women gave of themselves or of their time. On the contrary, later historians and enthusiasts have built upon Renaissance pride—and the attempts of Renaissance writers to cheer themselves up—a sunny, carefree, and perhaps slightly boring myth in which the people of fifteenth-century Italy are seen to have been bold universalists, individualists, optimists who entered the dawn of a new age with a warm glow of well-being, anticipation, confidence, and ease.

And yet, at night, in that model Renaissance city of Florence, five hundred years ago, nobody moved. The gates of the city were shut and locked. A curfew was imposed at sunset, and, after dark, only the police and government officials and the privileged few who had special passes stirred through the narrow stone streets, past the iron-barred windows and massive, bolted wooden doors. The only light in Florence at night came from the flickering oil lamps hung on the walls of houses to illuminate pictures of

On Renaissance Florence's only street of inns (opposite), travelers seek a night's lodging. The fleur-de-lis (inset above) had long been the city's emblem; it may refer to the name Fiorenza, the city built in a flowery meadow.

Visiting the imprisoned was one of many good works undertaken by members of the Confraternite, *brotherhoods pledged to put religion into practice. The* Confraternite *backed liberal elements in Florence and opposed the Medicis.*

protector-saints. Overhead in the alleyways, rude arches propped one tilting house against another, and occasionally there loomed a roughhewn towered house, a fossil of medieval Florence when families held off attackers by dumping boulders and boiling oil from the tops of their fortress homes. Dogs scavenged in the garbage, picking and choosing carefully. Ever since pigs, those omnivorous street cleaners, had been banned from the city, the thoroughfares had become filthier. The decomposed refuse left a glutinous slick on the paving stones, causing falls and fatal diseases.

At night the gates and doors of Florence were closed against thieves, murderers, marauders, and mercenary soldiers. Nothing could keep out famine, or the prolonged, implacable depression — and inflation — that buffeted Italy for centuries after the Black Death. In the 1340's the Black Death had ravaged Europe, destroying whole towns, cutting down fully one-half of the population of Florence. And, over the years, as the population would begin to increase, smaller epidemics of the bubonic plague would cut it back down, again and again, relentlessly, once every decade.

The old, familiar order was disintegrating with a savage pitilessness. Feudal barons lost their castles, and lands, and serfs. Prominent old banking families, among them the Bardi, Acciaiuoli, and Peruzzi, "the pillars of Christianity," declared bankruptcy, shaking the whole Florentine economy. The popes had become rapacious, worldly princes, entertained by crude buffoons and by comedies that toyed with sexual perversion. Old republican city-states came under the sway of mercenary captains or of shrewd, manipulative merchant-bankers who had put together novel capitalist enterprises, diversified companies that made factory wage earners of former artisans; and the influence and interests of the merchant-bankers extended ominously to other city-states and countries through octopine branch banks.

On an April night in 1478 the Archbishop Salviati dangled from a rope at a window of the government palace, the Palazzo della Signoria. Jacopo and Renato de' Pazzi had been hanged. A body floated down the Arno River. Nobody knew quite how this Grand Guignol had started. There had been some business competition between two families of merchant-bankers. Competition had been inflamed to a feud, feud led to murder, and murder led to vendetta. Before the vendetta had run its course, 270 Florentines had been killed, exiled, or financially ruined.

One serene, sunny day a horse broke loose in pursuit—so, at least, it was said—of a mare. Florentine shoppers, shopkeepers, merchants, fishmongers, and grocers ran in panic; market stalls were overturned; counters full of grain and corn were jostled and the produce scattered; shop fronts were abruptly shut; and the huge doors of the Palazzo della Signoria were bolted. The government magistrates thought that a revolution had broken out.

It was in this town that the Renaissance began.

The most striking, obvious change that had occurred in the Middle Ages was the growth of towns. The towns burgeoned, outgrew their original walls, were encased again in new, larger circles of walls, outgrew the enlarged circles, and finally grew—some would say sprawled—outside the confines of any walls at all. The change took many years, to be sure; and its very gradualness is a reminder of the difficulty of saying just when a historical phenomenon begins and when it ends. In general, however, the Middle Ages were a time of slow but steady growth toward a new urban civilization.

Then, from 1348 to 1350, the Black Death, one of the greatest and most terrifying catastrophes ever to strike the world, devastated Europe. Giovanni Boccaccio wrote in the *Decameron:*

The revered authority of both divine and human laws was left to fall and decay by those who administered and executed them. They too, just as other men, were all either dead or sick or so destitute of their families, that they were unable to fulfill any office. . . . The calamity had instilled such terror in the hearts of men and women that brother abandoned brother, uncle nephew, brother sister, and often wives left their husbands. Even more extraordinary, unbelievable even, fathers and mothers shunned their children . . . thousands fell ill daily and died without aid or help of any kind, almost without exception. Many perished on the public streets by day or by night, and many more ended their days at home, where the stench of their rotting bodies first notified their neighbors of their death. With those and others dying all about, the city was full of corpses. . . .

The Black Death riveted the attention of Europeans on the world around them. In the face of such calamity, one could pray, one could wait for heaven, one could pretend that what occurred was merely the transitory vale of tears through which one passed on the way to the real world of eternity. Or, one could turn on the material world, confront it, wrest its secrets from it, master it.

The Renaissance began when men and women turned on the physical world to subdue it. This turning, like the growth of towns in the Middle Ages, was not sudden, cannot be dated with any precision, but its effects were readily apparent. Not all Renaissance men and women were free of anxiety, not all were individualists or universalists, not all would have recognized the description given of them by Jakob Burckhardt, not all felt bold or irreligious, not all were Platonists or classicists, not all welcomed a new age—but almost all were materialists. They were not merely eager for things; far more than that, they believed in the material world the way their ancestors believed in God and heaven. They did not abruptly cease to believe in God and heaven, but they did begin to believe that the material world was their destiny, that the secrets worth knowing lay hidden in the physical stuff about them, that truth lay in nature, not on some spiritual plane, that the material world, not eternity, 7

was the "real" world. This change of consciousness was so vast, so revolutionary, and so convincing that we take it entirely for granted in our own times, and we cannot imagine how it could ever have been any different.

The change of mind—the invention, in effect, of the modern mind—was a potent motivator. In philosophy, the humanists revived Plato, who taught that there is an ideal world—and our own material world, the real world. When it came to art, Renaissance painters and sculptors investigated the laws of illusionistic perspective, labored for "realism," injected contemporary living people into ancient religious scenes, set biblical stories in contemporary settings (in which the olive trees were rendered with the exactitude any oil merchant could appreciate), and dissected cadavers by the dozen to see just what made men work. The poets wrote not in Latin but in their vernacular. The educators shoved aside theology and taught astronomy and navigation, anatomy, botany, and accounting. Mathematics textbooks were illustrated not with abstract diagrams but with pictures of Florentine merchants (How many bales of cotton does it take to make one bolt of cloth?).

When Luca Landucci, a Florentine apothecary, commenced to write his diary in the mid-fifteenth century, he began by listing the "noble and valiant men" (and no women) who were alive in his day. In his list he named an archbishop, a bishop, a doctor, a merchant-banker, several artists and sculptors, an organist—and two instructors of bookkeeping. The things of the world were put in lists, catalogued, inventoried, collected, counted. Diarists wrote elaborate descriptions of the furnishings in their homes, the food at banquets, the banners in a parade, the stalls in the marketplace.

The greatest collection of these collectors and listmakers and cadaver dissecters resided in Florence, which was, without doubt, the quintessential Renaissance city. Unlike the usual medieval towns that perched defensively atop

Seen across the Arno River, in this 1490 view Florence is enclosed by its walls and watchtowers. Rising within the city are the cathedral (capped by Brunelleschi's lofty dome), Giotto's slim campanile in front of it, and the tower of the Palazzo Vecchio at the right.

8

Italy's steep hills, Florence was brazenly settled in the unprotected valley of the Arno River, which powered the town's mills, supplied fish, carried away some sewage, and provided the vast quantities of water necessary to the washing and dyeing of the cloth on which the Florentine economy was based. The city was about two miles in diameter and was divided into two unequal portions by the river. It was surrounded still by walls, as most Renaissance towns were. The walls were surmounted by forty-five towers and perforated by guarded gates. The city's population had reached 100,000 in the fourteenth century, was reduced to 50,000 by the Black Death, and was never able to grow beyond 75,000 at the height of the Renaissance. Nonetheless, Florence was one of the half dozen or so largest cities in Europe, along with Naples, Paris, Venice, Salamanca, and Milan. London and Rome could barely muster 50,000 inhabitants in the healthiest of years.

Beyond the walls of the city lay the Tuscan hills, covered with vines and olive trees, farms and livestock. When Florence had a population of 100,000, it was said that its citizens consumed 100,000 pigs, sheep, and goats each year, about 4,000 head of cattle—and 70,000 quarts of wine every day. The foodstuffs were raised, for the most part, by tenant farmers who worked lands that were owned by townsmen. Despite the growth of the towns, Europe remained overwhelmingly pastoral, with about 85 per cent of the population living in the country or in small villages.

The farmers of Italy were a restless lot who moved around in search of a better share for their labor from farm to town, town to village, farm to farm. However much they moved, they usually had to settle for half the annual yield, and for a good deal of scorn from the city people. They were, said Alberti, "ploughboys who had grown up among the clods," and "all their efforts are directed at fooling you." Another landowner advised constant vigilance: "Never believe what you do not see, and never trust any of them." By law, peasants were worth only half a citizen, or townsman, and some peasants evidently hungered for city life, its riches and its privileges. "They are ill-bred churls," one Florentine sniffed, "puffed out with riches, who neither appreciated

good manners nor show courtesy to others, and whose only desire in life is to heap up gold, with which they vainly hope to ennoble themselves." It was not easy for a farmer to heap up gold, but it was possible; and in the Renaissance, strivers were offered a new sort of nobility of wealth rather than the old nobility of birth.

For the nouveaux riches, the country was transformed into a rough-and-ready idyll. The hills of Tuscany were adorned with eight hundred villas in which the well-to-do retreated from the summer heat, or the plague, worried their tenant farmers, planted new gardens bordered by civilized cypress, and talked of philosophy. "I have come here to my little villa," Cardinal Pietro Bembo wrote in a polished letter to a friend, "which has received me joyfully. . . . I hear no noise but that of some nightingales vying with each other around me, and many other birds who all seem to try and please me with their natural harmonies. I read and write as much as I want; I ride, walk, and often go for a stroll in the wood I have at the bottom of the garden. . . . I sometimes gather . . . a basket of strawberries in the morning. . . ."

For all this new-found romance of nature, however, the Renaissance was a thoroughly urban phenomenon. If men and women loved nothing better than to visit the country, none of them would deign to live there. Machiavelli, it is true, lived year-round seven miles south of Florence in a house—hardly a villa—at Sant'Andrea in Percussina; but that was because he had been implicated in an anti-Medicean plot and had to leave town. He hated the country. He spent his afternoons, he wrote to a friend, at a local inn, "where I usually find the landlord, a butcher, a miller, and a couple of brickmakers. With these I act the rustic for the rest of the day, playing at *cricca* and *tricche-trach*, which lead to a thousand squabbles and countless exchanges of insults—our fights are usually over a farthing, but we can be heard shouting nonetheless from San Casciano. So, trapped among this vermin I rub the mould off my wits and work off the sense of being so cruelly treated by Fate—" by sitting down in the evenings to write *The Prince*, which Machiavelli hoped would win him the attention of the Medicis, and an invitation to return to the city, where one could talk of politics and art and

SCALA

history and business and be in the center of life.

Every morning at dawn the city gates were opened to the farmers to bring their produce into the market, and they entered in a scramble of carts and donkeys and horses. Nothing echoes noise like narrow stone streets lined with stone houses, nor do Italians seem to be a naturally reticent people when they wish to make themselves heard. The Renaissance must have been a shatteringly noisy time. The farmers entering town would have headed directly for the central place, or piazza, where the Old Market was set up. Just as all roads led to the Forum in ancient Rome, the jumble of Florentine streets radiated from the Old Market piazza. Commerce, not religion or politics, lay at the center of Renaissance towns. Two other piazzas provided eccentric centers: that of the cathedral and that of the government's Palazzo della Signoria.

The closeness of the streets would not have

Clothes are handed out to the needy by members of the **Buonuomini di San Martino.** *This fraternity took special care of poor gentlefolk, notably including those ruined by the Medicis.*

seemed odd to the farmers; they would have known that the densely packed houses provided shade in the suffocating summer and that it was easier for citizens to build barricades against invaders in narrow streets than in wide boulevards. And, for all their filthiness, the streets of Florence were regarded as a prime symbol of progress: they were paved, and most of them were well drained, and many of them boasted sewers—this at a time when London still had muddy roads.

Almost all of the buildings had shops on the ground floors. Shopkeepers lived above their stores, and in the mornings they opened the shutters of their windows, let down a hinged shelf, put out their wares, and conducted busi-

11

ness. Clothing shops might be concentrated on one street, blacksmiths on another, but, for the most part, the city's neighborhoods were organized not by trade but by family. The first generation of a family to settle in town would establish its household, and successive generations would live nearby, banded together for protection and support in business, politics, and the vendetta. Thus the Medicis dominated one neighborhood, the Strozzis another, rich and poor relatives and allies of various trades commingled and intermarried.

The walls of a house might form the walls of its neighbor; gardens were shared. Sons lived with fathers, brothers divided family homes, and when the Sassettis divided their house, they inadvertently gave one room away to the house next door. When Messer Pagolo Vettori decided to write out in his diary just which rooms in his house were his own and which were his neighbor's, he found he could not do it.

During the Renaissance, however, the Florentines engaged in a paroxysm of building: a hundred new palaces went up in the fifteenth century. Without the money, the laboring population, the sense of a secure future, of the freedom from internal and external violence and war, the Florentines commenced a building program that was not even remotely matched in inspiration or magnitude anywhere else in Europe. Designed according to classical ideals of aesthetics, the new palaces were extraordinarily commodious. The ceilings were so generously high that a three-story palazzo was as tall as a six- or eight-story building of the twentieth century. And they were wide and deep: two dozen buildings were torn down to make room for the Strozzi palace. Replete with private inner courts and spacious gardens, these new palaces were nothing less than private monuments, testaments to family immortality in this, not the next, world.

On June 24, the feast day of Saint John, the city's patron saint, Florentines in their finery cheer on their favorites as

On July 10, 1489, according to Landucci's diary, "they began to bring gravel to make the foundations of the Palazzo of Filippo Strozzi. . . ." By August 20 Landucci was getting impatient: ". . . all this time they were demolishing the houses, a great number of overseers and workmen being employed, so that all the streets around were filled with heaps of stones and rubbish, and with mules and donkeys who were carrying away the rubbish and bringing gravel, making it difficult for anyone to pass along. We shopkeepers were continually annoyed by the dust and the crowds of people who collected to look on. . . ."

Thus the farmers and their donkeys were joined in the streets by the construction workers, gravel carriers, shopkeepers, dogs, merchants, women on their way to early Mass, the previous day's drunks who had slept in the taverns rather than risk violating the curfew, workers in the wool and silk trades, barbers, fishmongers, poultry venders, beggars, thieves, astrologers, whores, and an odd feudal baron or two who did not yet realize that they were anachronistic. Modern cities provide no such mix of urban crowds or urban odors. In addition, to the aroma of fish, chickens, sewage, garbage, horses, fresh pears and figs and fava beans, people of the Renaissance had each other. It was Michelangelo's father who advised, when his son set out for Rome, "Stay away from the baths, but scrape yourself from time to time."

Each morning this horde crushed into the piazza of the Old Market to patronize the grocers and street barbers, engage in an occasional shouting match or a stabbing, and see who else was up and about. Life in Florence was a public affair. Shopkeepers thrust themselves and their shops out into the streets, not merely because their houses happened to be small, but because they needed to be in the midst of the action, the gossip, the potential business connections.

young riders gallop full tilt down stone streets in a madcap race for glory that ended, for some, in broken bones.

Our beautiful Florence [one native bragged to a Venetian] contains within the city in this present year two hundred seventy shops belonging to the wool merchants' guild, whence their wares are sent to Rome and the Marches, Naples and Sicily, Constantinople and Pera, Adrianople, Broussa [Brusa], and the whole of Turkey. It contains also eighty-three rich and splendid warehouses of the silk merchants' guild, and furnishes gold and silver stuffs, velvet, brocade, damask, taffeta, and satin to Rome, Naples, Catalonia, and the whole of Spain, especially Seville, and to Turkey and Barbary. . . . The number of banks amounts to thirty-three; the shops of the cabinet-makers, whose business is carving and inlaid work, to eighty-four; and the workshops of the stonecutters and marble workers in the city and its immediate neighborhood, to fifty-four. There are forty-four goldsmiths' and jewellers' shops, thirty goldbeaters, silver-wire-drawers, and a wax-figure maker. . . . Sixty-six is the number of the apothecaries' and grocer shops; seventy that of the butchers, besides eight large shops in which are sold fowls of all kinds, as well as game and also the

native wine called Trebbiano, from San Giovanni in the upper Arno Valley; it would awaken the dead in its praise.

The author of this little panegyric to Florentine prosperity was, like Ficino and Bruni, incurably cheerful. In a civilization that is coming apart (or, as we say at a comfortable distance, reconstituting itself) much news is simultaneously good and bad. A society filled with contradictions makes self-contradictory news, and one could as easily view this list of shops as a lament. The wool business, which was the foundation of the Florentine economy, was unraveling. The silk business was struggling to replace it, and would never succeed in doing so. The number of banks had been three times as great a hundred years earlier; and the list of goldsmiths, jewelers, goldbeaters, and silver wiredrawers is one of those disturbing signs of a concentration on luxury goods for a diminishing market, charac-

Babies whose parents could not afford to keep them and babies born to slave mothers in affluent households were left at an orphanage called Santa Maria degli Innocenti. Here they are being cared for by the staff of wet nurses.

teristically a last-ditch stand of an economy in retreat. And, as for Trebbiano, it is hard to believe that it would ever have awakened the dead in its praise.

In sum, however, the sense of insistent striving, and the interminable listing and counting up of shops and things and money, was pure Rennaissance poetry.

The riches of Florence were based, throughout the Renaissance, on the declining wool industry —as the most casual glance at its streets would show. Along the river were the pens and racks for dipping fleece. The wool was first washed in water mixed with ammonia, then scoured in great vats, lifted out, drained, rinsed in the Arno, hung out to dry, combed, oiled, carded, spun and wound by women and girls—and then sent on to the weavers, dyers, finishers, and folders. There was the Street of Shearers, the Street of Cauldrons, and the Road of Dyers—the Corso dei Tintori. In the streets back from the river, most houses were fitted out with iron brackets at the windows, which supported wooden bars, from which hung pieces of cloth. "Indeed," as one historian has written, ". . . Florence appeared to be one vast drying and stretching ground. Cloth of all kinds and colors waved in great lengths in every quarter, and imparted an extraordinary aspect to the streets."

Perhaps a third of the population worked in the wool business; they worked from sunrise to sunset (with one hour for one meal in winter, two hours for two meals in summer), six days a week, fifty-two weeks a year, with fifty-two Sundays and forty other holidays off for recreation. Only one-fifth of the working population were privileged to belong to guilds; the other four-fifths were truly, formally, and forthrightly downtrodden. "Let the working masses and the humblest sector of the middle classes struggle for the good of the Republic," one of the more enlightened humanists of the day wrote. "Those that are lazy and indolent in a way that does harm to the city, and who can offer no just reason for their condition, should either be forced to work or expelled from the Commune. The city would thus rid itself of that most harmful part of the poorest class. . . . If the lowest order of society earn enough food to keep them going from day to day, then they have enough." From time to time

the most harmful part of the poorest class took up paving stones and rose in futile revolt.

A third of the Florentine population were classed as paupers and so excused from paying taxes. Of this third, a good many were employed as servants. Good servants were, of course, hard to find; Michelangelo maintained that all servant girls were "whores and pigs." The servant population was very slightly augmented by slaves—mostly Tartars from around the Black Sea area, as well as some African blacks and Shakespearean Moors. In one ten-year period, in the flourishing Venetian slave market ten thousand slaves were sold.

The remainder of the population was distributed among occupations that can be roughly identified by the major and minor guilds around which business was organized. As with so many other institutions, the guilds were disintegrating in the fifteenth century—economic and political power had come to be increasingly concentrated in the hands of wealthy merchant-bankers—and the guilds had come to resemble less vital trade associations. Nonetheless, they continued to provide an index of relative status and power. The minor guilds represented the manual laborers: blacksmiths, shoemakers, tanners, saddlers, locksmiths. By the fifteenth century, the oldest of the guilds, that of the carpenters, had been shunted down the order of precedence to occupy the undistinguished position of next to last. At the very bottom of the order of precedence was listed the trade that remained closest to agriculture, the Guild of Bakers. The Renaissance rejected the feudal agrarian society of the past with a vengeance.

The Wool Guild, the Silk Guild, the Guild of Furriers and Skinners, the Guild of Bankers and Moneychangers, were among the seven major guilds. These were the guilds of the nascent industrial capitalism that had supplanted the old agricultural economy of feudalism. To take care of the legal problems of this new order there was the Guild of Judges and Notaries—and, for the ever-present problems of health, the Guild of Doctors and Apothecaries. At the top of the list of these major guilds, however, was the Calimala, the guild that dealt specifically with the dyeing and finishing of foreign cloth. It was in this guild that one found the leading Florentine fam-

SCALA

ilies, the rich few who built the new palaces, retreated to country villas in the summer, and whose names are still to be found today on streets and piazzas and in history books: Alberti, Albizzi, Bandinelli, Bardi, Capponi, Corsini, Frescobaldi, Guicciardini, Medici, Pazzi, Peruzzi, Pitti, Pucci, Ricci, Ridolfi, Rucellai, Strozzi, Tornabuoni. And, if one crosses the list of the Calimala members with the list of the Guild of Bankers, one discovers the names of those who ran the government: the Albizzi, Guicciardini, Strozzi, Pitti, and, most notably, Medici—always with a little help from their friends.

Twelve oligarchs formed the Signoria, which provided Florence with its executive bureaucracy, for the administration of taxes, the regulation of trade, and so forth. Because the Florentines were chary of surrendering their destinies to any board of governors, the members of the governing committee, the Signori, were shuffled with hasty regularity: their terms of office were a scant two months long. In addition, government powers were divided among the Signoria and its chief executive, the gonfalonier, the podesta (the chief judge), and the *capitano del popolo* (the head of the militia). And the powers of the Signoria were constantly broken up, rearranged, checked, and frustrated by the Council of Three Hundred, the Council of Ninety, the Council of the Heads of the Seven Major Guilds, the Council of Good Men. In case of war, or other crisis, a special commission, a *balía,* was given temporary absolute powers. The fragmentation and complexity of this system made it possible for the government not to work at all. Thus, while the Signoria provided the appearance of republican government, an oligarchy ruled efficiently behind the scenes, led by one or another of Florence's powerful families.

It was the conceit of Florence that all men were equally citizens, all wore the same clothes and the same "citizen's cap." The conceit was necessary, perhaps, to bring down the old feudal barons from their privileged stations. But, one can spot the Medicis in the crowd. All men wear tights and a simple tunic and the same cap, and the same soft leather boots or shoes, and, in cold weather, the same cloak. All women wear the same, simply cut full-flowing dress with a tight bodice and a high neckline. (Both sexes wore a discreetly hidden piece of fur to provide a gathering place for bugs.) But, in the city that made its fortune on cloth, and in which anyone could tell dozens of different grades of wool, the tunics of the privileged few had a telltale fringe of fur around the cuffs and collar, a particular fineness of texture, a smoothness, a softness, a brilliant clarity to the color. On feast days or for portrait sessions, the tunic might be of white silk brocade, stitched with gold thread. And the Medici and Strozzi and women of the other oligarchs wore dresses of white or cerulean silk, set off by a single strand of matched pearls.

These were the people who commissioned the artisans of the lower classes to decorate the walls of their new palaces with paintings, who hired scribblers to translate Plato, and who bore witness to the fact that chaos demands, willy-nilly, new forms.

Other Italian cities differed from Florence: Ferrara was ruled by old-money aristocrats, Venice by an exceedingly tightly knit oligarchy, Naples by a king, Milan by a dictator. Ambassadors from these other towns attracted attention in the streets of Florence. The men of Lombardy wore brightly colored and snugly tailored clothes; the Bolognese wore multicolored, and embroidered, hose; the Romans all seemed dandified. The ambassadors represented cities whose economies were based on munitions, or mining, or shipping.

The experience of life in the Renaissance was not uniform throughout the Italian peninsula; it was not the same in city and country, nor among all the social classes, nor was it the same for both women and men. Nonetheless, most Italians shared very much the same experience of living in a world that was chaotic, violent, anxiety-ridden, plague-struck, superstitious, depression-wracked, fiercely materialistic, repressively governed, exploitative, discriminatory, filthy, and dangerous; and it was out of these base materials that those with the greatest nerve—or, as Alberti called it, will—made the Renaissance.

The Florentine sense of style is exemplified by this servant, painted by Ghirlandaio. Like many other people shown on these pages, she is a figure in a painting of a biblical scene—in this case, **The Birth of St. John the Baptist.**

16

CHAPTER II

AT HOME

When Luca da Panzano drew up an inventory of his most important personal possessions, he recorded his furniture, his linens, his clothes and other expensive items, and one piece of paper on which his family tree had been sketched. The continued possession of all the other items in Luca's inventory depended upon a proper attentiveness to his family tree.

Each individual owed his first obligation to his family: to his own household of his father, mother, brothers and sisters, uncles and cousins, and servants; to his uncles and cousins who lived next door or on the same street or around the same square; and to the extended family of his neighborhood, his relatives by marriage, his friends and his allies. In the mid-fifteenth century in Genoa four hundred men bore the name Doria, and many more embraced the Dorias' causes as their own. This family, which resembles a modern Mafia "family" at its broadest extent, was obliged to defend every individual member. A crime committed by a Doria against anyone was a crime committed by the Doria family against the other's family, and the subsequent retaliation

In the close-knit families of Renaissance Italy children like the little girl in the fresco opposite were treated with affection and dressed as adults. At home, they often had pets such as the dog and cat shown in the inset above.

pitted family against family.

The head of the family was the father—or to distant relatives and allies, perhaps the godfather—and his decision about a business investment, a marriage contract, the building of a house, the purchase of a farm, was accepted as final. His decision was usually made, however, after consultation with brothers, uncles, cousins, and perhaps sons.

Women were not consulted in any matter of importance. The best one might say of a woman was that "her understanding was superior to her sex," and it was not often said. Alberti wrote the basic text on the Italian family, *Four Books on the Family*, in which he observed that the first objective of family policy was to produce male children and the first duty of women was to bear male offspring. One must not, it was said, allow a wife to "have the bridle, but keep it always in your hands, and control her, never letting her gain any point, and using her sometimes with spirit, sometimes with a delicate hand, just as one does a sparrow hawk, so that she does what you want. And make her love and honor you, and not resent your harshness."

The historian John Gage quotes the advice a Florentine woman gave to her daughter: "Never touch the box or purse or other place in which [your husband] keeps his money, so that he may not suspect you; and if it so happens that for

19

any reason you do touch it, do not take anything, but put it back carefully. . . . If on the arrival of some honorable person, you are busy with some menial housekeeping duty, quickly put away your distaff and spindle, and hide your menial work, whatever it may be, so that you will not look as if you were brought up on a farm. . . . Also I command you to be discreet, and not to desire to know too much, nor to give heed to soothsayers, nor to their witchcraft and incantations, for it is most unseemly for women to know as much as men about masculine affairs."

The best a father could do with a female child was to have her married to advantage. An impoverished aristocratic family might use a daughter to gain a son of an up-and-coming merchant family; a nouveau-riche family might arrange to have a daughter marry into an old aristocratic family. The Orsinis, a noble Roman family, acquired a connection in this way to the new wealth of the Medicis; and the Medicis parlayed the distinction into Catherine de' Medici's mar-

riage into the French royal house. Women thus became one of the vehicles for social mobility—helping, by their arranged marriages, to balance and transfer economic and political power. All Renaissance Italians were busy matchmakers, and none were busier than the rulers of the city-states, who made and blocked marriages with a keen appreciation of the advantage or threat any marriage might hold to their power.

To be a desirable marriage prospect, a young woman had to be possessed of a dowry, especially if she were to bring only money, and not social status or political connections, to her mate. The less well-to-do patriarchs of Florence built up dowries for their daughters by investing in the state dowry fund, which, like a bond, accumulated interest. If a man had many daughters, he might send some of them to a convent, in order to keep his dowry savings from being spread too thinly. When a girl reached the age of fifteen or sixteen, her father's investment and its accumulated interest dictated his prospects for his daughter. Investment in the fund was heavy, and it provided extra dividends for the government. If a girl died, her father's investment in the fund belonged to the city. The fund accounted for half of the revenues of Florence, and it financed much of the municipal building, streets, hospitals, sewers, and wars.

No negotiation was more important than the negotiation of a marriage contract, and it might take months or years to conclude. A respectable dowry for a merchant's daughter amounted to about 1,000 florins in the fifteenth century, a good dowry, 1,500 florins—most of it in cash, some of it reckoned as the value of clothes and other possessions the bride brought with her. One could buy a female slave for 50 florins, a mule for 10. The rental for a house in the middle of Florence was about 25 florins a year, for a house on the outskirts 10 florins, for a slum dwelling 1 or 2 florins.

With a dowry of 1,000 florins, a young man could buy a quarter interest in a silk or wool shop, on which he would earn as much as 15

Well-to-do people, like this pair, enjoyed sumptuous repasts, but for most of their fellow citizens the day's two meals were nearly always meatless—and nutritionally inadequate.

per cent, or 150 florins a year. If he combined his wife's dowry with funds put up by his brothers and cousins, he could get into the trade in foreign cloth, join the Calimala, work his way into the Signoria, evade his taxes with the impunity government office bestowed, and become a distinguished citizen.

A dowry had to be handsome, then—but not too handsome. One Florentine, Giovanni del Bene, described a different sort of problem with the wedding arrangements for his nephew. The bride's father was asked to post a bond of 2,000 florins in case the wedding did not go through. "The rumor which has spread of the large dowry which I have given has ruined me and done great harm with respect to my taxes . . . ," the bride's father complained. "Concerning this bond of 2,000 florins, everyone will think that I provided a dowry of that size, and this will be my destruction."

Once the negotiations for marriage had been completed, a number of the relatives of the prospective bride and groom were assembled in

The central market, where grocers, butchers, and fishmongers kept booths or stalls, was the busiest place in town—and, with the hawking, bickering, and general din, among the noisiest.

church along with the intermediaries who had drawn up the marriage contract; the representatives of the two families confirmed the agreement by shaking hands—thus the name of the first ceremony of marriage, *impalmare*. (In licentious Rome the relatives all kissed, and so the ceremony was known as *abboccamento*.) The bride did not appear at the *impalmare;* she appeared at the second ceremony, the betrothal, and then again at the third ceremony, which was held in her home. On this occasion a good many relatives and friends were invited to witness the exchange of vows and rings and to join in the wedding feast. When Lorenzo de' Medici was married, the feast lasted from a Sunday until Tuesday at noon, and the guests consumed, among other things, 800 calves, 4,000 chickens, 5,000 pounds of sweetmeats—and 100 kegs of wine a day. When a Sforza was married to a

Bentivoglio in Bologna, houses were torn down to widen the streets and make room for the wedding feast.

A standard wedding feast consisted of a first course of ravioli made of herbs, chopped pork, and cream cheese in a thin pastry, fat-fried and rolled in powdered sugar; a second course of meat, often veal; and a third course of a great pie made, as a descendant of the Niccolinis has written, with "pork, chicken, ham, onion, herbs, parsley, dates, almonds, flour, spices, saffron, cheese, eggs, sugar, and salt." For a suitably spectacular centerpiece, a pie pastry might be baked, with a filling of semolina to maintain its shape; after it was removed from the oven, little windows were cut in the top of the pastry shell, and a large hole was cut in the bottom to remove the semolina. Through the hole in the bottom, the cook would put—if the pastry shell were large enough—four and twenty live blackbirds.

Daily fare was a good deal simpler than a wedding feast, to be sure. The very poor ate bread and a thin vegetable soup and tasted meat only a dozen times a year. Milk and butter and good cheese appeared on the tables of those who were slightly better off. Most households, even of the well-to-do, had meat only on Sundays. Breakfast consisted of bread, fruit, cheese, and various jams. The main meal was composed of a salad, bread, fruit, cheese, soup, an occasional bit of sausage, vegetables, and substantial amounts of pasta. The varieties of soups and pastas provided a good range of tastes; and the fruits (the grapes and pears and melons and figs), combined with the assortment of cheeses, gave the daily menu a sensation impossible to duplicate after the invention of refrigeration. The fact that Italians celebrated a holy day almost every week provided frequent excuses for one of the dozens of veal dishes, and for stews and roast chickens, pigeons, pheasants, trout, and more sausages. One often hears of wealthy Renaissance Italians with weight problems.

After the wedding feast, the bride and groom were taken to a bedroom in the house of the bride's father, and the marriage was consummated. A witness to the bedding down of Anna Sforza and Alfonso d'Este in Ferrara recorded that "we stood talking for awhile, and then the bride and groom were put to bed, and we all went up with them right to the bed, laughing with them. On the don Alfonso's side was the Marquis of Mantua with many others who taunted him, and he defended himself with a piece of stick; it seemed strange to both of them to see so many people around their bed, all saying some pretty thing as they usually do in these cases. We left, and the following morning we . . . found they had both slept very well, as indeed we believed they ought to have done." Next, the bride and groom attended the celebratory Mass of the Union, and finally the groom took his bride to his home.

The elaborateness of the succession of marriage rituals resembles the cautious procedures that attend corporate mergers or alliances between nations, and, in theory at least, the marriage might break down at any moment until the groom took the bride home. Often, the bride's family would pay the promised dowry on an installment plan, and, equally as often, the groom suspected he would never receive the final payment. Paolo Niccolini, a merchant in the Wool Guild, procrastinated for three years between the *impalmare* and the *nozze*, the day he took his bride home. "During this time," he wrote, "I received the dowry in many installments and at many times. On the day I took [my bride home] some of it was still owing to me. I was not satisfied with so many small sums, and this was the reason I waited so long to take her, because I wished to have the dowry first, to avoid quarrels."

When a well-to-do man brought his new bride home, he would, according to Alberti, lock the door and show his wife "all the things of value, the silver, the tapestries, the fine clothes, the gems and the places in which they were all kept. For I did not wish any of my precious things to be hidden from my wife . . . only my books and papers, and those of my ancestors did I keep locked and hidden, then and thereafter, so that she should neither read, nor even see them. . . ."

Niccolini's wife, Cosa Guasconi, joined a going household. A slave named Lucia served as Niccolini's mistress and bore him two sons before Cosa arrived in the house. The year Cosa was installed, Lucia gave birth to a third son. Paolo and Cosa had eleven children, of whom six died in infancy and one in her teens. Paolo bestowed a dowry of 1,770 florins on his only surviving daughter. One of his sons was married to a Portinari (a Medici business associate) with a dowry of 1,800 florins; another son, much to Paolo's chagrin, became a monk.

After Cosa and Paolo had been married for twenty-eight years, Cosa died; Paolo himself married the widow of a Portinari and had five more children. His second wife brought a dowry of only 900 florins—including the value placed on her four dresses (one green, one purple with silver hooks, and two white), two gowns (one black, one reddish-brown), thirteen wimples, thirty kerchiefs, six embroidered shirts, one veil with forty-one pearls, one cap, two purses of drawn gold, one hat of purple velvet, a brocade needlecase, two pairs of ornamented scissors, a cloth of Arras decorated with green foliage and two unidentified figures, an illuminated Book of Hours, and one boiler and two pots, weighing forty-six pounds. By the time Paolo's second wife arrived in the Niccolini house, the master had added a fourth illegitimate child, the daughter of a widowed friend, to his retinue.

The sexual mores of the Renaissance are somewhat obscure. Women were most certainly expected to be virgins before marriage, remain ever faithful to their husbands, and have no duties other than to raise their families and be supportive of their husbands. Men were presumed to be licentious and to be free to pursue sexual liaisons outside marriage. Among the well-born, the harmless, mannered flirtations of courtly love provided one of the favored divertissements of poets and courtiers, but it was unthinkable to "dishonor" a woman. Or was it? There can be no doubt that sexual mores were undergoing an extraordinarily radical change: paintings and statues of nudes abounded; beauty, handsomeness, and vitality were greatly praised; adulterous affairs were often spoken of, and casually spoken of, even among the well-born who were thought to have honor to lose. The Renaissance does indeed appear to have been a vigorously libidinous era, and, if women were still far from liberated, they did begin to have extramarital affairs, and were grudgingly accounted by some men to be civilized, if not quite equal, beings. Sex was not at all a taboo subject, and sexiness—both male and female—was

A popular book advised "cooking once a day only in the morning" for the poor, to save fuel; but the kitchens of the well-off were busy all day with activities like cheese-making (above).

widely admired in their lives and their art.

Still, the Renaissance was a male-dominated society, and illegitimate children and slave-mistresses doubtless took their toll on Renaissance households. Alessandra Strozzi complained of a slave of hers: "It is an incredible thing how ill she has behaved to me and to [Alessandra's daughters]. She is so perverse that no one can do anything with her. She treats me as if I were the slave and she were the mistress." And yet Alessandra could not sell the slave for fear that the embittered woman would start ugly rumors about the Strozzi girls and ruin their marriage prospects.

Family members may well have felt an urge to get away from one another. The new palaces of the fifteenth century, with their many large rooms and high ceilings, may have been built to proclaim status, but they also simply gave families more space to get away from relatives, and even with the new spaciousness, heads of households pushed their relatives out of their houses. Whereas brothers, cousins, and uncles once commonly shared homes, in the fifteenth century a bride often insisted, between the

23

impalmare and the *nozze,* that her husband buy out the shares that relatives owned in his house. The new palaces came more and more to house A good many Renaissance men and women viewed this disintegration of traditional family arrangements as an ominous social symptom. Only determined optimists discerned in the change a movement toward enhanced privacy.

Very little space of the new palaces was actually devoted to living quarters. A fourth, or sometimes a third, of the space was left open: the ground floor (itself taken up by shops and storage areas) opened onto an internal courtyard; the top floor opened onto a loggia. The family lived for the most part in the dozen or so rooms on the middle floor. The number of rooms did not much vary from palace to palace; larger palaces simply had larger rooms. There were no corridors, and one room opened into another. The central gathering place in an Italian house, except for the rich, was the kitchen, which served also as dining room, family room, card and game room. There were only two meals a day, at ten in the morning and five in the afternoon, but a glowing olivewood fire burned all day in the fireplace, which was large enough to walk into. Houses were built to stay cool in summer, not to be warm in winter; except in the homes of the very rich, there was little glass for the windows, and the cold was kept out by closing the shutters; the kitchen fire provided warmth and light.

Furnishings were sparse. Chairs and tables were novel; formerly, residents and guests sat on chests, stools, or on the edges of beds, and tables were improvised by placing a board on trestles. In the fifteenth century tables and chairs could be found in well-to-do households; in wealthy homes, they were often handsomely carved. Rushes covered the floor, making a place for vermin to breed. Paolo Niccolini had one Barbary carpet, which was placed on the steps leading up to his bed.

The bed was by far the most impressive piece of furniture in the house. Two mattresses (weighing 295 pounds) and four down bolsters (weighing 92 pounds) were set on the wooden frame of Paolo's bed, and mulberry twigs may have been put under the bed to attract the fleas. The bed was fitted out with sheets and blankets, covered by a canopy, enclosed by a curtain, and surrounded by a bench with drawers under the seat, a smaller bed for a child or servant, a stand for towels and odd clothes as well as hats, a chest or two, a board and trestles, a small, three-legged stool or two, and, at the head of the bed, hanging on the wall, the cloth of Arras decorated with foliage and two figures.

Elsewhere in the house were beds for the children, a few plain chests, some candlesticks, wash basins, crockery, mugs and metal (not glass) cups, six pewter plates, and a case containing eight knives. The inventory of Paolo's household goods does not mention forks or spoons, but forks were beginning to be popular during the Renaissance. They were used to transfer food from a common bowl or platter to individual plates. Husbands and wives shared the same plate. They ate with their fingers, which they wiped on the tablecloth. Paolo had two white silk tablecloths, embroidered "in the Paris fashion," two tablecloths with azure stripes, and two small tablecloths with borders—perhaps of crimson or black stripes—at the ends. He also had 12 small napkins, which was uncommonly civilized of him.

One other household item was remarkable— the *cassone,* or wedding chest, in which the bride had brought her clothes and other possessions. The *cassone* was sometimes painted with brightly colored scenes of wedding feasts and constituted, after the bed, the showpiece of the house.

Renaissance houses had very little else of any value in them. Some, to be sure, might have tapestries on the walls and some decorations such as paintings or statues, but these were not worth a great deal. An inventory of Medici possessions lists a number of paintings and sculptures. Not many of these are identified by the name of the craftsman or artist, but two paintings by Masaccio are valued at 12 florins for both; a painting by Pollaiuolo is valued at 20 florins; Andrea del Castagno's painting of Saint John is valued at 15 florins; one by Filippo Lippi, 10 florins; an imported piece by Jan van Eyck, 30 florins; a Fra Angelico, 12 florins; a Giotto, 6 florins; to another Giotto, no monetary value was attached.

Historians have debated for more than a century the connection between economics and the

SCALA

This view of a nobleman's death (left) and funeral procession (right) illustrates a manuscript of Aesop's Fables. When a member of one of Florence's great families died, people of all classes stood in the streets to watch the cortege wind slowly past on its way to the cathedral.

the jewelry, the antique cameos and gems, pitchers and goblets ornamented with silver and gold, and ancient manuscripts and illuminated prayer books. The new printed books that were beginning to open up extraordinary possibilities for the spread of learning and that did so much to nurture the Renaissance were reckoned as valuable for their information, but were considered worse than worthless as objects; indeed, those accustomed to hand-copied and painted books considered printed books some sort of vague threat to civilization itself, with the thought that mass production somehow cheapened the contents of the books.

One other item on Paolo Niccolini's inventory deserves attention: "24 towels, 12 fine and 12 coarse, and 6 little towels for the head." The Niccolinis probably depended primarily upon rubbing and scraping to keep themselves clean, but they evidently bathed from time to time. In the Middle Ages, Italians bathed at public baths; by the fifteenth century, anyone who frequented

the public baths was accounted a whore or a wastrel. Most Renaissance houses had a small, portable tub for bathing; to conserve hot water, family members often bathed two at a time.

The wealthiest families rarely had more than two or three servants in most Renaissance homes. In a dukedom such as Milan, where the ruling family of Sforzas mingled private servants with the retinue of their official court, the line between servants and government retainers is somewhat blurred. And the Medicis at one time had a household numbering fifty, of whom only fourteen were members of the immediate family. In most bourgeois homes, however, a few servants were thought sufficient to do the cooking, washing, and cleaning; and many families took in young girls, saw to their education, and after ten years or so provided them a dress and a gown and a dowry of 50 or 60 florins.

Letters between husbands and wives speak of children with the sort of unaffected warmth Italians usually show for children, both their own and of others. Letters from Medici children to their fathers report on games and jokes and progress in studies, and beg the head of the house to return from business trips, or take a vacation from city politics to join the family for a vacation at the summer villa.

Piero de' Medici, age six, wrote this letter from one of the family's country villas to his father Lorenzo in the city: "I write this letter to tell you we are well, and although I do not as yet know how to write well, I will do what I can. I shall try hard to do better in the future. I have already learned many verses of Virgil, and I know nearly the whole of the first book of Theodoro [a Greek grammar book] by heart; I think I understand it. The master makes me decline and examines me every day . . . I commend myself to you . . . ."

At age seven, Piero wrote in Latin to his father: "Lucrezia [his sister] and I are trying who can write best. She writes to grandmother Lucrezia, I, to my father, to you. The one who obtains what he asks for will win. Till now Lucrezia has had all she wished for. I, who have always written in Latin in order to give a more literary tone to my letters, have not yet had that pony you promised me. . . ."

A seven-year-old's wish for a pony—and the manner in which he pursues his desire—cannot seem too uncommon. But here is the same seven-year-old remarking on the business that keeps his father in town: "The war as far as I understand goes in our favor this year, but we do not quite understand how the sword that wounded us

is to be broken if only the sheath is hit. . . . We only hope for peace through victory. Scipio is to be driven to Carthage in order to get Hannibal out of Italy. We beseech you, we your children, to have the more care for yourself the more you see that the enemy rather lays hidden snares than dares open warfare. . . ." It is just possible that Piero was aided in the composition of this letter by one of the household guests at the villa that summer—his tutor Angelo Poliziano, one of the more renowned poets of the Renaissance.

Later that summer Piero wrote, "That pony does not come. . . ." But the boy favored his father with some news anyhow: "We are all well and studying. Giovanni [age three] is beginning to spell. . . . Giuliano laughs and thinks of nothing else; Lucrezia sews, sings, and reads; Maddalena knocks her head against the wall [alarming news], but without doing herself any harm; Luisa begins to say a few words; Contessina fills the house with her noise. All the others attend to their duties, and nothing is wanted to us save your presence. . . ."

Still later in the summer, Piero wrote, "I fear that some misfortune has happened to that pony. . . . I think of it night and day, and until the pony comes I shall have no peace. . . . For, as I have already written to you, I am here on foot, and sometimes it is necessary for me to go in the company of my friends. . . ."

At last Piero wrote his father, "I cannot tell you, Magnificent Father, how glad I am to have the pony, and how his arrival incites me to work. . . . He is so handsome and so perfect that the trumpet of Maronius would hardly suffice to sing his praises. You may think how I love him; particularly when his joyous neighs resound and rejoice all the neighborhood. . . . I send you many thanks for such a fine gift, and I shall try and repay you by becoming what you wish."

Children were meant to play, to be shielded from the worries and harshnesses of the grown-up world, and to work hard at their studies in preparation for the time when their presumably carefree days would end. They attended school for four to six hours a day and went to work or to a university at age fifteen. The student population of Florence was very large, perhaps as high as 7,500 in the mid-fifteenth century. Students were meant to learn grammar and

arithmetic, the tools of a merchant, and that was all. The principal tools of instruction were the abacus and the rod. Exceedingly few youngsters were instructed, as the Medici children were, in Latin and Greek, logic and philosophy.

Above all, the impression conveyed by diaries and letters of the Renaissance is that home and family were necessary bases for men, but that men spent little time at home. Shopkeepers, industrial workers, and farmers spent long hours at their work, and then long hours talking in the streets and squares and taverns. Men of the merchant-trader class were often out of town on affairs of business or politics. Women spent their time in church, at home, with their children. Men were powerful, and absent.

In 1470 Paolo's brother Otto, age sixty, had a household made up of one bastard son of his own, two bastard sons of his twenty-two-year-old son, his pregnant second wife, and children aged 24, 22, 18, 17, 16, 13, 12, 11, 8, 5, 4, 3, and 1½. Otto, a lawyer, was away in Rome on diplomatic business. In the autumn his wife Bartolomea supervised the wine making at Otto's farm outside Florence. In the spring she tended to the silkworms. By April she was exhausted. The tutor for her five-year-old son Lodovico had suddenly departed. ("I knew he was not what Lodovico needed," Bartolomea wrote to Otto, "because he had less brains than a goose.") She required Otto's consent to her new plan for a tutor—for fathers, however distant from their homes, demanded to know everything about their children and took an especially keen interest in the education of their offspring. Older children wrote to their fathers, and their fathers wrote back. One of Otto's boys, incidentally, showed how the Catholic Church was losing its

hold on youngsters' minds during the Renaissance: the boy hoped his father would return home soon; and to hasten his father's return, Otto's son prayed to "the gods."

"I wish you would return," Bartolomea wrote to her husband, "these long sojourns of yours weary me," and, "it seems to me that you intend to remain a year [in Rome], and I can never say how it hurts me." And then, "I have need of you."

Otto's brother Paolo wrote, too, advising Otto to return to Florence. Financial troubles seem to have been plaguing the family. Otto's son Piero had been somehow extravagant, and Paolo had had to give him some avuncular advice until Piero's eyes "rained tears." Paolo then lent Piero some money so that the young man could straighten out his financial difficulties, but that was not the only problem the family had. Bartolomea asked Otto repeatedly for a new coat; she was ashamed, she said, to go out of the house in the shabby coat she had. Next time, Bartolomea said, she must be left better provided for.

That September, Otto died in Rome. He had settled his debts with his tailor, his doublet-maker, the shoemaker, the butcher, the linen merchant, the miller, grocer, carpenter, and ironmonger, but the records do not show that he bought a new coat for his wife before he died.

The building of new houses, the quest for comfort and privacy, the education of children, the acquisition of books or cameos or other symbols of new success and status, the accumulation of dowries for daughters, the financing of new businesses in a tumultuous economic era, all required a constant flow of money. "Let us contemplate the needs of private life," a Florentine said. "Where are our houses and palaces procured. . . ? From riches! Whence come our clothes. . . ? Whence the meals for us and our children? From riches! Whence the means to educate our children and make them virtuous. . . ? From riches!" Those who did not have riches borrowed them—and so set going the economic engine of the modern world.

The good taste of wealthy patrons and the talents of artists and craftsmen transformed the domestic scene. Four-poster beds with ornately carved headboards were common, and exquisitely wrought objects—mirrors, vases, candlesticks—relieved the severe lines of the furniture.

CHAPTER III

MERCHANT-BANKERS

The salt that the Niccolinis used at their table came from the territory around Florence; the mineral alum, used to fix the bright dyes in their woolen clothes, came from papal mines at Tolfa. Wine and wheat, wood and stone, were local products. For centuries these basic commodities and a few others had sufficed for most needs of food, clothing, and shelter. Throughout Italy most trade was a local affair, carried on among neighboring towns.

The revival of commerce in the late Middle Ages began along the rivers, and first favored such river towns as Florence, the towns along the Po River, and, elsewhere in Europe, the cities of the Rhine and the Rhone. Then, as trade grew to a more sophisticated, intercontinental business, the seaport cities of Genoa, Venice, and—through the nearby port of Pisa—Florence became the great centers of trade along with Lisbon, Cádiz, London, Antwerp, Alexandria, Beirut, and the inland depots of Damascus, Aleppo, and Bursa. Wonderful profits were to be made in all these dealings. A two-year voyage to the Far East and back, with a vessel carrying a diverse cargo, could return as much as 3,000 per cent profit on the original

In ships like the ones opposite, landlocked Florence carried on, by way of various ports, trade that enriched its merchants—who profited, too, from dealing in the currency accepted everywhere, their own gold florin (above).

investment—if the ship did not sink. More secure investments were available, too, to those who had the capital. The merchant Agostino Chigi cornered the market in alum. He bought control of alum mines of Naples, stored the alum in Sienese ports—and waited for the prices to go up.

Manufacturing, trade, and market manipulation all called for substantial amounts of cash, or credit, and so it was that banking enterprises sprang up. Church strictures against usury were skirted by the grander capitalists with remarkable ease. Although interest could not be charged for loans, moneychangers could exchange florins for ducats or ducats for gulden and profit from the different rates of exchange in different locales. With more than five hundred currencies in use throughout Europe (in itself a symptom of the wonderful confusion of early capitalism), opportunities for exchange were manifold. The Guild of Bankers was called the *Arte del Cambio*, and bankers maintained the conceit that they were mere moneychangers. To finance a voyage to Egypt, a banker would advance florins for a specified period, and insist on ducats in payment. The difference in exchange rates could be as high as 20, 30, or even 40 per cent.

In order to minimize the risk attendant upon such ventures, men of substance often engaged in both trade and banking, thus establishing themselves as merchant-bankers. As merchants,

31

they diversified as much as possible, engaging in both the wool and silk trade, combining the manufacture of armor and weapons with trade in spices, and loading ships with varied cargoes of low-priced bulk goods such as alum, and high-priced high-risk shipments of spices. As bankers, they protected themselves by laying off part of their risk with partners, and by taking out in-

been shattered, in part, by an upsurge of genuine democratic sentiment, and genuinely republican governments had been established in dozens of Italian towns in the twelfth and thirteenth centuries. Gradually, the rich and powerful acquired the dominant influence in these governments. The death rattle of republicanism occurred in Florence in 1378, when the cloth-

surance. So cautious were the bankers that they often took out insurance on the lives of rulers, in case the death of a prince would harm trade.

Inevitably, merchant-bankers became embroiled in politics. To obtain a trading license or mining rights, or to ensure the political survival of a sympathetic prince, a merchant-banker might have to make a loan to a ruler. Politics was the riskiest business. The Bardi and Peruzzi banking families had gone into bankruptcy primarily because of uncollectable loans they had made to kings and princes. Nonetheless, the rewards could also be handsome: half of the Medici banking profits and most of the Medici working capital came, in the mid-fifteenth century, from the papal court in Rome.

Rich men had a potent motivation, then, to become not only merchant-bankers but merchant-banker-princes. Business could be threatened by ambitious rulers of other states or by disgruntled employees at home. Feudalism had

workers shut down all business, burned the palaces of a dozen aristocratic families, rioted, looted, lynched a police official, and were finally quieted by a "reform" government. The reform government was cautiously, and very slowly, taken over once again by the wealthy, who were careful to keep numbers of artisans and small shopkeepers in public offices, but to so arrange the selection of candidates for office as to ensure a government of loyal supporters.

The oligarchy was in turn closely controlled by several leading families, and those leading families were beholden to Cosimo de' Medici, whose family, between 1434 and 1471, spent 663,755 florins "for charity, buildings, and taxes." Had Cosimo not controlled the government, his business rivals would have, and might well have taxed the Medicis out of business. A generation later this wisdom was confirmed. When Cosimo's grandson Lorenzo was twenty years old, his father died, and, as Lorenzo disingenuously recorded it, "The principal men of the city and of the State came . . . to encourage me to take charge of the city and of the State, as my grandfather and father had done. This I did, though on account of my youth and the great responsibility and perils arising therefrom, with great reluctance, solely for the safety of our friends and possessions. For it is ill living in

In the fifteenth century, a single family, the Medici, rose to economic and political dominance over Florence. The Medicis' wealth and power were based on their banking operations. The façade at left is that of the Milan branch. The bank's fortunes peaked in mid-century under Cosimo de' Medici, (below), with branches in all the great cities of Italy and in London, Bruges, Geneva, Lyon, Basel, and Avignon.

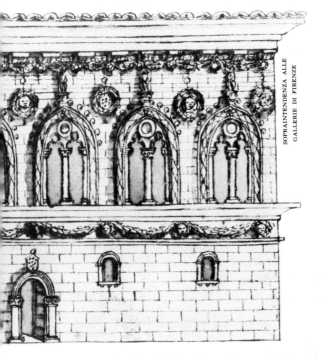

Florence for the rich unless they rule the State."

In theory, Florence had a graduated income tax. In practice, the government ran so constantly at a deficit that it had to borrow money continually from its wealthiest citizens (paying up to 16 per cent). In consequence, small taxpayers paid taxes that went in large measure for interest payments to the rich on their government bonds. In 1457, for example, Gino Capponi paid the eighth highest tax in Florence: 64 florins. At the time he paid his tax, he had already received two of his three annual interest payments on his government bonds: 315 florins. Government, like wool manufacturing and banking, was a paying business.

The Medici family is the best known of the merchant-prince dynasties. Their origins were obscure, but their name suggests that the first notable Medici was a doctor, perhaps one who built up a trade and a good income from the outbreaks of plague. The family coat of arms bore five *palle*, or balls, and it may be that they represented pills. Giovanni di Bicci de' Medici, who was eighteen years old at the time of the clothworkers' revolt, was the first Medici to enter banking in a significant way. It was Giovanni di Bicci who established the Medicis as bankers to the Vatican. Cautious, shrewd, painstakingly modest, Giovanni di Bicci advised his descendants: "Never strive against the will of the people, unless they advocate a baneful project. Speak not as though giving advice, but rather discuss matters with gentle and kindly reasoning. Be chary of frequenting the [government] Palace, but rather wait to be summoned. . . . Be as inconspicuous as possible."

The most accomplished merchant-prince of the Medici family was Giovanni's son Cosimo, who was born in 1389, took over the family bank in 1429, and forged the political machine that ruled Florence—inconspicuously—from 1434 until his death in 1464. In his teens Cosimo developed a

33

passion for the Greek classics, and for the idea that merchant-princes should resemble Plato's philosopher-kings and use their wealth in the pursuit of knowledge, refinement of the spirit, and grace.

Cosimo was married to Contessina Bardi—whose shattered family banking interests had been absorbed by his father—and was sent to travel in Germany, France, and Flanders before being put in charge of the Medici branch bank in Rome. This sort of apprenticeship was standard for the sons of established businessmen, and the young men were expected to acquire a knowledge of foreign businesses, products available for import, some fluency in languages, an understanding of foreign weights, measures, tariffs—and of other businessmen. The young men made contacts, formed judgments of branch managers, gauged the strengths and weaknesses of competitors—and incidentally spread the ideas of the Renaissance.

Cosimo's introductions were in especially good order, and he tended to move in exalted circles. He was, Pope Pius II said, "Of fine physique and more than average height; his expression and manner of speech were mild; he was more cultured than merchants usually are and had some knowledge of Greek; his mind was keen and always alert; his spirit was neither cowardly nor brave; he stood up easily to hard work and hunger." And he had a quick and cutting wit. When an upright churchman suggested that priests should be forbidden by law to gamble, Cosimo countered with the suggestion: "Begin by forbidding them loaded dice."

Back in Florence, Cosimo embarked on his political career at a time when Rinaldo degli Albizzi led the Florentine government, and took Florence into a war of conquest against the neighboring town of Lucca. After several inconclusive and expensive years of war, Albizzi settled for peace, and Cosimo let it be rumored that he thought Albizzi had bungled the war. In September of 1433 Cosimo was summoned to the Palazzo della Signoria and incarcerated in a room at the top of the palazzo's tower. His family prevented his execution by calling on well-placed business associates in Rome, Ferrara, and Venice to put in a cordially threatening word with the Florentine oligarchs, and by giving the gonfalonier 1,000 florins. ("They were stupid," Cosimo said of the gonfalonier's clique, "for they might have had 10,000 florins or more. . . .") Cosimo was exiled to Venice, from where he conducted his business and continued to mix money and politics.

Within a year, Albizzi had lost his following

As a center of manufacturing, Florence imported materials, as at left, from sources near and far. A third of its citizens worked at making textiles, producing 70,000 bolts a year. Above: the emblem of the wool manufacturers' guild

34

in Florence, and elections in the Signoria commenced to go against him. Elections worked like this: the Signori were not "elected" in our sense of the word; they were, rather, chosen by lot every two months. In this way, it was assumed, no one could rig the government. What, after all, could be less subject to human manipulation than random selection of officers? The insiders controlled only one element in this: names of Signori were drawn by lot from a purse, or *borsa;* the insiders were the ones who chose which names were to be placed in the *borsa.*

Unfortunately for Albizzi, however, the system had a flaw: between the time names were placed in the *borsa* and the time names were drawn out, people could change their minds. Suddenly, in the autumn of 1434, a number of Albizzi partisans chosen by lot turned out to be Medici supporters. How much it cost Cosimo to change these minds was not recorded, but Cosimo was recalled from exile. After his return, Cosimo stayed in the background of the government, refusing even to serve on the committee of electors. But this did not prevent him from acquiring superlative distinctions: he became the richest man, with the most political power and the biggest banker of his time, possessed of the largest library and surrounded by the brightest scholars. He paid the highest taxes and evaded even more; he was, of all Florentines, the most intimately acquainted with rulers of other states; his children made the best marriages; and he lived in a palace that was, by the standards of his fellow oligarchs, the most inconspicuous in town.

The grandest palace in Florence was built by Luca Pitti—or at least it was begun by Luca Pitti. After Cosimo's death, Luca tried to seize control of the government from Cosimo's son Piero. Luca failed, his partisans were exiled, and he was ruined. His palace remained unfinished; workmen refused to do anything for him; and the pretentious Pitti palace was not completed until many years later by others. "You follow the infinite," Cosimo is supposed to have said to Luca, "and I the finite; you lay your ladders in the sky and I lean them close to the earth lest I may fly so high that I may fear to fall."

Cosimo was not often seen in the streets of Florence or at the Palazzo della Signoria. He worked in his studio at home. To the branch

In the great trading center that was Florence moneychangers—ready to exchange florins for the coins of Venice, Genoa, Milan, or any of the European states—performed an essential role.

banks in Geneva, Venice, and Rome, Cosimo added Medici banks in Ancona, Milan, Pisa, London, Bruges, and Avignon. He made between 20 and 30 per cent on his money, collecting tithes for the pope, manufacturing wool and silk, trading in brocades, silks, jewels, and silver plate, making loans, underwriting insurance, entering partnerships in short-term ventures, acting as agent in purchases of such commodities as ginger, dealing in tapestries for wall hangings and chair coverings, making quick trades on horses, a brass chandelier, a bed, and one hundred bales of almonds, dealing in large quantities of iron and alum, and recruiting soprano choir boys in Bruges for St. John Lateran at Rome. All of this activity called for fast communication, and communication was fast enough. It took between three and six days to reach Rome and Genoa from Florence by sea, six days overland from Florence to Milan. Goods and travelers moved most quickly and safely by

water. Overland, by way of the remains of ancient Roman roads, travelers moved in packs to guard each other from highwaymen.

That these early days of capitalism depended upon a measure of improvisatory skill is evident from the career of one of Luca Pitti's ancestors who set out as a young traveling apprentice, took up professional gambling, parlayed his winnings from French aristocrats into high-risk investments in horses and wine, made loans to others who had been embarrassed in gambling ventures, and finally fetched up back in Florence with enough money to buy a large share in a cloth business. Bankruptcy was at least as common a story as success. Ships sank, caravans were robbed, agreements were broken, and—the greatest source of business failure—debts went unpaid. Renaissance Italians invented not

only modern capitalism, but also double-entry bookkeeping, with its easily manipulable assets and liabilities, accounts receivable and accounts payable—and credit. As the merchant-bankers were learning, the neatest trick of all that capitalism allowed was the huge and complex debt structure, which in turn demanded a growth economy and constant material progress, and which occasionally shook out those who were overextended.

In the fever of speculation, branch managers sometimes indiscreetly embezzled company funds to take to the gaming table or rashly loaned money to a king who later simply canceled all his debts, or died. Wars could upset trade, and so could plague. If a merchant found himself on the wrong side of a political dispute in a foreign country, he might discover that his goods had

This fresco, **The Effects of Good Government,** *allegorically sets forth a Renaissance ideal: benevolent despotism. Siena thrives beneath the hovering figure of Security, whose banner reads, in part: "Without fear may everyone travel freely and each man work and sow."*

been confiscated or that political influence had caused him to be excommunicated by the pope. If he had his goods stored in another town, he might find that the town had been sacked by bandits or by a mercenary army. He had, therefore, to keep on the right side of Italian and foreign politicians and princes and kings and popes, of the weather, of his own business associates and family; and he had to have a grasp of the value of hundreds of commodities and currencies, all without the benefit of a large staff or of computers. To become rich, and remain so, required an array of talents that very few mastered. There were perhaps two hundred such men in Florence, and of them all, Cosimo was the richest, at least four times wealthier than his nearest rival.

It would be surprising if men of such an active and inquiring cast of mind did not turn to investigate the curiosities of scholarship and the arts. A friend of Cosimo's, Niccolò Niccoli, neglected his business altogether to devote himself to collecting and studying books, and when he died (predictably bankrupt), Cosimo acquired his library and began to add to it. Cosimo hired a local book dealer, Vespasiano da Bisticci, to build his library, and Vespasiano hired forty-five copyists who turned out two hundred books in less than two years.

Some of these books were immediately useful

37

to a merchant and landowner: they dealt with plants and medicine, techniques of farming and building, the customs and terrain of distant lands with which Cosimo traded. But utility was not as potent a motivation as a sheer hunger for knowledge. Late in his life, Cosimo discovered a young student of Greek, Marsilio Ficino, and set the young scholar up on a farm outside Florence. There Ficino spent all of his time, at Cosimo's behest, translating Plato. This interest in Plato led to the establishment of an informal Platonic Academy, of which the leading Florentine scholars became members, and which met from time to time with Cosimo to discuss urgent questions of justice, the immortality of the soul, the reconciliation of pagan Greek and Christian wisdom.

Perhaps it was out of a sense of nostalgia, perhaps from a need to escape an unbearable present, perhaps from a wish to bury the recent feudal past, that Italians turned so avidly to the classical past. Whatever the reason, they thought they could do no better than to give rebirth to the ancient world—and, of course, the knowledge they brought back to life transformed the world. The merchant-bankers were not alone in inspiring this rediscovery of the past, but, by gradually usurping the role of the Church as patron of the arts and scholarship, they did much to secularize intellectual endeavor and to turn

Bookkeepers, such as the one shown above, kept the accounts of the city's enterprises. Among the most important of these was the wool trade. On the page above, taken from a textbook used by one of Lorenzo de' Medici's young sons, a problem in arithmetic is illustrated by a scene of merchants trading wool for cloth.

it to the concerns of mastering the material world.

Once he had completed his apprenticeship travels, Cosimo did not often move out of Florence. He stayed at home, surrounded by the constant company of business associates, architects, philosophers, poets, politicians—and members of his family. When he received ambassadors from Lucca, they were astonished by his behavior:

The audience was held in his own house, according to custom, and during discussions a small child, his grandson, came up to him with some oatsticks and a little knife for Cosimo to make him a whistle. Cosimo signified that the discussion was adjourned, devoted himself to the child and made the whistle, telling him then to run away and play. The ambassadors were somewhat offended. "Sir Cosimo, we are surprised at your behavior. We have come to you on behalf of our commune to treat of grave matters, and you desert us for a child." With a laugh Cosimo flung his arms round their shoulders. "My brothers and lords, are you not fathers, too? Don't you love your children and grandchildren? You are surprised that I should have made that whistle; it's as well that you didn't ask me to play it. Because I would have done that, too."

In a society in which money is so important—and where pursuit of it is seen to imperil one's very soul—spending is never casual. Cosimo spent money to rebuild the sacristy of San Lorenzo in Florence, the abbey at Fiesole, and the monastery of San Marco in Florence. He provided San Marco with a library of four hundred books, and commissioned Fra Angelico to paint religious scenes to decorate the walls of the monks' cells. He reserved one room at the monastery for himself, where he could go at any time to meditate. In that room Fra Angelico painted the *Adoration of the Magi.* "Only have patience with me, Lord," Cosimo reportedly said, "and I'll balance our books."

Cosimo had three villas, including one at Cafaggiolo, which he especially liked because, he said, all that he could see from its windows he owned. When he was there, he pruned vines every morning for two hours and then retired to his study with a book.

He attended Mass every morning in his private chapel, which Benozzo Gozzoli had decorated with a painting of the *Journey of the Three Magi.* The Magi were one of Cosimo's favorite subjects for paintings, and he commissioned paintings of the kings again and again. The three reminded him, no doubt, that he was himself a powerful ruler, and also that he owed ultimate homage, as did the kings, to God. Cosimo was not a completely modern godless man; he was a transitional figure. At the top of some of his business ledgers was the motto: "In the name of God and of profit."

He was too bright, and too tough-minded, to be fooled by his own ruses to get around Church strictures against usury, and he evidently worried a great deal that he was on his way to hell. He sought out the most old-fashioned and rigidly moralistic churchman in Florence, the Archbishop Antonino, and talked with Antonino repeatedly and at length about usury. When Antonino came to write his *Summa Moralis,* he included five chapters on usury, in which he said that it was acceptable for bankers to take a percentage on bills of exchange, because of the assistance such bills afforded travelers, and in ventures in which capital was used to finance an enterprise. Antonino's pronouncement must have been a relief to Cosimo.

He died in 1464 at the age of seventy-five. When he lay on his deathbed with his eyes closed, his daughter was alarmed and, it is said, asked Cosimo anxiously why he closed his eyes. He replied, "to accustom them to the dark." After his death, the Florentines referred to him as *Pater Patriae,* and it appears—however much it may offend our own republican sentiments—that the Florentine people did prefer to be ruled by a benevolent despot rather than try at republican government. Perhaps they had seen self-rule collapse too many times under the onslaught of competitive families who were ever ready to sacrifice public interest to private gain. In the famous Renaissance painting of *Good Government and Bad Government,* there is no hint in the panel on *Good Government* of public forums for public speech, of elections by citizens imposing their will on rulers. *Good Government* represents prosperous shops, fertile fields, tradesmen setting out on a tranquil road, bourgeois comfort, peace, and prosperity.

The merchant-bankers did much to transform the world and their fellow men's sense of reality. They eliminated famines by moving grain from place to place; they substituted silk for woolen clothes; they conjured riches out of bookkeeping; they turned cloves and nutmeg into banks, alum into factories and houses and churches. They turned a republic into an oligarchy, and election by lot into a system of predictable corruption. With the use of Socratic dialogue, they turned an incorruptible churchman into a defender of usury and a graduated tax structure into a profit center for the rich. They made the natural world a place for civilized discourse; they made the Vicar of Christ on earth a source of working capital; and they changed the ideal of beauty from modest Madonnas to nude Davids and Venuses. From the most trivial item of daily life to the most profound ideas of ultimate truth, the merchant-bankers proved themselves powerful manipulators of ideas and things. If many of their activities were merely those of aggressive getters and spenders, it is also true that the merchant-bankers displayed wonderfully agile, modern minds. They possessed, the best of them, a fluidity and resiliency of intellect, a sure grasp of facts, a passion for novelty and experiment, and a certain exhilarating daring.

CHAPTER IV

WAR AND VIOLENCE

When the imperatives of the Renaissance family encountered an opposing Renaissance passion for wealth, the result was often predictably violent. Pope Sixtus IV, a Franciscan who bargained his way shrewdly into the papacy, had as great an ambition for his family as any other Italian. Although he lacked legitimate sons and daughters, he had no shortage of nephews and presumed bastard sons. Among his nephews was Girolamo Riario, a dim and pliable young man, on whom Sixtus determined to bestow a state carved out of the papal territories northeast of Florence, in the part of Italy known as the Romagna.

The Romagna is beautiful, mountainous country that opens onto the Po Valley and the Adriatic Sea. Across it ran the Florentine trade route to Venice and the East. To ensure continued passage through the Romagna, Lorenzo de Medici attempted to cut the pope's new state in half by offering to buy the town of Imola from the duke of Milan. The duke of Milan at first agreed to sell Imola to Florence and then, tempted by an enhanced offer from Sixtus, agreed to sell the town to the pope instead for 40,000 Venetian ducats, a sum almost equal to the same number of florins.

Armed assaults (opposite) occurred often in Italian streets. The same magnates who patronized art and science hired thugs to further their private schemes or frustrate those of rivals. Inset above: a soldier's helmet and dagger

Sixtus, who had no money of his own, had sought a loan from the establishment that had for so long served as bankers to the pope, the Medici branch bank in Rome. When the Medici bank procrastinated, Sixtus turned to its principal rival, the branch bank of another Florentine family, the Pazzi. The Medicis ceased to be bankers to the pope, and Sixtus was enabled to buy Imola.

But the Medicis were not to be so easily shoved aside. Francesco de' Pazzi was informed that a new, retroactive law regarding intestacy had been passed. Whereas the Pazzi family had inherited money from the Borromeos, by way of a daughter's marriage, the new law provided that this money must go to another Borromeo relative—who was, as it happened, a friend of the Medicis. Thus the Pazzis were stripped of the capital to carry on their banking business. Meanwhile, in the papal town of Città di Castello, a revolt against papal authority broke out, led by Niccolò Vitelli, with support from Lorenzo de' Medici.

Sensing danger, Sixtus entered into alliance with King Ferrante of Naples. Florence had allied itself with Venice and Milan. Thus the major southern powers were arrayed against the major northern powers, and so they remained, tensely and cautiously, until Easter Sunday, April 26, 1478, when the Pazzis resorted to murder in hopes of regaining their power. On

41

that morning Lorenzo and his brother Giuliano were persuaded to attend Mass at the Florentine cathedral in the company of Francesco de' Pazzi. Machiavelli recorded what followed: "The murderers being ready, each in his appointed station, which they could retain without any suspicion, on account of the vast numbers assembled in the church, the prearranged moment arrived and Bernardo Bandini, with a short dagger . . . struck Giuliano in the breast, who, after a few steps, fell to the earth. Francesco de Pazzi threw himself upon the body and covered him with wounds; while, as if blinded by rage, he inflicted a deep incision upon his own leg. Antonio and Stefano the priest attacked Lorenzo, and after dealing many blows, effected only a slight incision in the throat; for either their want of resolution, the activity of Lorenzo, who, finding himself attacked, used his sword in his own defense, or the assistance of those by whom he was surrounded, rendered all attempts futile. They fled. . . ."

Luca Landucci made this entry in his diary: "Meanwhile all the city was up in arms, in the piazza and at Lorenzo de Medici's house. And numbers of men on the side of the conspirators were killed in the piazza, among others a priest of the bishop's was killed there, his body being quartered and the head cut off, and then the head was stuck on the top of a lance, and carried about Florence the whole day. . . ."

The Pazzi War had begun, and its causes were interestingly diverse. Once materialism came to be the dominant myth of the modern world, most historians would discern economic motivations as sufficient *casus belli* for all wars — and there is no doubt that commercial competition motivated a great deal of violence during and after the Renaissance. But the Pazzi War was caused by Sixtus for reasons of dynastic ambition, by the Pazzis out of a desire for wealth and power and from a sense of wounded honor, by Lorenzo de' Medici for the sake of Florentine trade routes and personal political power; and, finally, the Pazzi War was caused by sheer violence welling up in thousands of Florentines who rampaged and murdered for reasons that can only be explained by psychology.

If rumors got around that a merchant was hoarding grain, riots broke out. If a town suffered from a genuine grain shortage, granaries were

stormed. Word of a new tax could lead to the looting of shops. Gambling led to many fights with daggers. To venture out of the house at night was to court death, and to travel without the company of a well-armed band of friends was equally foolhardy.

In certain districts of Italy [Burckhardt wrote] where civilization had made little progress, the country people were disposed to murder any stranger who fell into their hands. Heads of state were so often assassinated that a prince or Pope rarely died without accompanying rumors of foul deeds. The Borgias were well known for their white powder poison; Caterina Riario tried to murder Pope Alexander VI with a poisoned letter; plotters against Pope Leo X tried to kill him by persuading his physician to treat him with poisoned bandages; physicians to Alfonso of Naples told him not to touch a book given to him by Cosimo de Medici for fear of poison. Nor did princes hesitate to practice various forms of violence on their subjects. . . .

"It is not only the Court of Rome," Burckhardt said of Sigismondo Malatesta of Rimini, "but the verdict of history, which convicts him of murder, rape, adultery, incest, sacrilege, perjury and treason, committed not once but often. The most shocking crime of all [was] the unnatural attempt on his own son Roberto, who frustrated it with his drawn dagger. . . ."

An urge for violence lay always ready to be tapped — and that simple urge provided the connective links among intimate, personal murders, stabbings, riots, family feuds, intracity battles, and the most flamboyant display of its fruits in spectacular interstate wars. Renaissance Italians had a positive passion for bloodletting. There can be no other explanation for the extravagant retaliation against the Pazzis, for the quartering of the bishop's priest, for the parading of his head on a lance point, or for what Landucci reported of the fate of Jacopo de' Pazzi's dead body: ". . . some boys disinterred it . . . and dragged it through Florence by the piece of rope that was still round its neck. . . . And when they grew tired and did not know what more to do with it, they . . . threw it into the river. . . . And it was considered an extraordinary thing . . . because children are usually afraid of dead bodies. . . . And as it floated down the river, always keeping above the surface, the bridges were crowded

Especially south of Florence, on the roads to Rome, travelers risked being robbed and slain by bandits, including out-of-work mercenaries. Such crimes were common; note, in the picture, the woodcutter's indifference to the murders.

with people to watch it pass. . . ."

Among those caught in the maelstrom was the Archbishop Salviati, and his murder permitted Pope Sixtus to employ a favorite Vatican device: he excommunicated Lorenzo de' Medici and some members of the Florentine Signoria. The Florentines presently countered with the layman's favorite device against popes: they called for a council to reform the Church. And Sixtus replied by dispatching armies to the field under the leadership of Alfonso, duke of Calabria, and one of the most famous condottieri of the period, Federigo da Montefeltro, duke of Urbino.

Federigo was one of the aristocrats among the condottieri. He was not merely a free-lance mercenary warrior who drifted about the country-side looking for war, or stirring it up. He was a professional soldier who made his living from war; but more than that, he was himself a prince who maintained his own little state of Urbino. Burckhardt wrote of him: "Feeling secure in [Urbino] where all gained profit or employment from his rule, and where none were beggars; he habitually went unarmed and almost unaccompanied. . . ." He would take "his frugal meals in an open chamber, while Livy, or in time of fast-

OVERLEAF: *In this panel from Paolo Uccello's* Rout of San Romano, *the Florentine commander, Niccolò da Tolentino, leads the attack against the Sienese. Most of the "Florentine" soldiers were mercenaries.* 43

ing some devotional work was read to him. In the course of the same afternoon he would listen to a lecture on some classical subject, and thence would go to the monastery of the Clarisses and talk of sacred things through the grating with the abbess." A learned man, a patron of the arts, Federigo had one of the most refined courts in Europe, all supported by the proceeds of war.

He was recognized throughout Italy as the leading condottiere of his time. He was often

S. ANASTASIA, VERONA

The decaying corpses of hanged men, left dangling from gibbets as a warning to anyone who might flout the laws or defy the authority of a local despot, were a common sight in Italy.

overly cautious; he was not the most imaginative tactitian; but he was prudent and dependable, and his soldiers were well organized and generally well controlled. While he did not frequently bring off brilliant victories, neither did he too often lose. And he led his own troops into battle, unlike other soldier-princes, who rented out their armies and stayed home themselves.

In the mid-fifteenth century, there were about one hundred and seventy condottieri, each of whom led two hundred or more "lances," the basic three-man unit of the cavalry. Of those one hundred and seventy captains, only a handful stand out as great (or greatly disastrous) generals: Federigo da Montefeltro; Sigismondo Malatesta, a brilliant and unpredictable leader; Bartolommeo Colleoni, the Venetian captain general whose insanely fierce visage was captured in the famous equestrian statue by Verrocchio; the Milanese Alessandro Sforza, who, when Florence fell into arrears on his pay, seized a Florentine merchant caravan; Jacopo Piccinino, who, suspected of some treachery by King Ferrante of Naples, was strangled by one of the king's Moorish slaves; and a few others.

Most city-states had their own citizens' militias, but few of these militias were sufficient, or sufficiently trained, for times of real crisis. Thus the city-states hired mercenaries—most of them Italians, a few of them foreigners—on a contractual basis. Contracts specified monthly pay, length of service, anticipated bonuses, and treatment of booty and prisoners. By the time of the Pazzi War, contracts were customarily signed for a period of six months to a year, with an option clause for renewal. As recently as the fourteenth century, it had been common to let condottieri go at the end of a war, but that practice had many drawbacks: footloose bands of soldiers turned into marauding bands of thieves in peacetime, endangering the lives of farmers, of travelers, of merchants on the road, and entire small towns. In the long run, it seemed cheaper and safer to keep the soldiers under contract year in and year out; thus, by the mid-fifteenth century, permanent, professional military establishments had come into existence. Some were maintained by such large city-states as Venice and Milan; others formed the economic basis of small principalities such as Federigo's Urbino;

still others were kept by renewing their annual contracts and were lent or rented to other city-states as the need arose. Occasionally successful condottieri would be rewarded by the gift of a fortress or a town, a practice that gave the condottieri places to keep themselves and their troops in time of peace.

The condottieri recruited, equipped, and trained their troops, and charged stiff fees for their services. Micheletto Attendolo once demanded a contract from Florence that required an advance payment for salaries and equipment of 45,000 florins, for which Attendolo promised to bring into battle 600 lances and 400 infantry.

The traditional three-man lance consisted of a heavily armored man-at-arms, an armored aide, and a page. The man-at-arms fought, the other two fed him and cared for his horse and armor. In the latter half of the fifteenth century, the five- and six-man lance was coming into vogue. Heavier armor for the man-at-arms required more elaborate assistance to get him on his horse—and spare horses had to be brought along, since the tremendous weight of armor rapidly wore out mounts. These lance groups were organized into twenty-five lance squadrons, and eight or ten squadrons were organized into columns. In battle these columns resembled massed tanks, and they were sent crashing headlong to smash and scatter first the enemy cavalry and then the enemy infantry. The cavalry charge was a fearsome shock tactic of the set-piece battle. It ended, usually, in a bloody melee, leaving the field littered with dead horses and helpless men-at-arms—a great waste of expensive animals and armor. For that reason, among others, condottieri tried to avoid the set-piece battle that was such fun to watch but such a drain on the budget.

The infantry, cannon fodder then as now, was recruited by the condottieri from among the poor, the criminal, the potentially criminal, and the unashamedly vicious. In the fifteenth century, this rabble was beginning to acquire some status, to be led by members of upper-class Italian families, and to take on the structure of the three-man lance, with one fighting man commanding aides. Some fought hand to hand with sword and shield, some were armed with crossbows, and some carried handguns that were several feet in length. (In the Pazzi War two

thousand of the ten thousand Milanese infantry troops carried handguns.) The harquebus was not yet, but soon would be, in fashion.

The artillery units were the ones that lugged the huge cannon around the mountainous peninsula. It required more than one thousand oxen to move the Milanese artillery, which consisted of sixteen guns. Lighter cannon were used in field battles, and heavier cannon were reserved for siege warfare. They all made a dreadful noise,

SCALA, ALINARI

Sigismondo Malatesta, lord of Rimini, who had himself painted in this pious pose, was the most ruthless of tyrants. Pope Pius II called him "the disgrace of Italy and the infamy of our times."

which frightened both men and horses; but they appear to have made no other contribution to military affairs except to slow down an army on the march.

Armies fought in the spring and early summer and the autumn. Late summer was too hot (especially under a full suit of armor), and winter was too cold. They rarely fought on Sundays or holy days. And, because battles were so vicious when they did occur, the armies spent most of their time trying to avoid fighting at all.

In 1478 Federigo da Montefeltro led the papal troops into the southern end of the broad, marshy Chiana Valley south of Florence. As he moved toward Florence, he seized, or marched over, the tiny fortress towns of Castellina and Radda. It would seem that Federigo was protecting his rear by taking these two towns, but the strategic considerations could not have been too compelling. Castellina and Radda were, at the same time, militarily insignificant and viniculturally interesting. Some of the better Tuscan wines (particularly the reds) come from the neighborhood of these two towns, and Federigo probably stopped by to pick up some wine.

He then turned abruptly west to the Elsa Valley and the forbidding Florentine fortress of Poggio Imperiale. This fortress was militarily important; raiding parties could well be sent out from it to harass Federigo's troops. It was, also, a rock of a fortress, with thick, sloped walls that could withstand the worst artillery attack, and with supplies that could enable its defenders to hold out for a very long time. On the other hand, if Federigo succeeded in taking the fortress, it was only a fortress, with none of the rich spoils that smaller towns offered. After looking at Poggio Imperiale for a time, Federigo turned his army around, went back to the Chiana Valley, and laid siege to another wine-producing town, Sansovino.

Landucci recorded some details of the opening phase of the war, noting some other small towns that Federigo overran: "23rd July. They captured Rincine and destroyed it, and took away men and women of all classes. . . . Each day there was some incursion or other, and the enemy overran Panzano, pillaging and burning. . . ."

The Florentines took to the field under one of the most incompetent generals of the fifteenth century, Ercole d'Este of Ferrara. According to Landucci, "Our men made an incursion into the territory of the Sienese, and pillaged and burned the mills and captured on various occasions more than 100 horses. . . ."

". . . The enemy took Lamole [excellent red wine there], and captured more than 100 persons. . . . The rule for our Italian soldiers seems to be this: 'You pillage there, and we will pillage here; there is no need for us to approach too close to one another.' "

As the countryside was laid waste and famine spread, so did its companion: "At this time the plague had increased so much, that 40 or more were sick at the hospital, and 7 or 8 died every day, and some days even 11. . . ." And then a few days later—for it was a characteristic of the disease to spread like a brush fire—"there were between 60 and 70 sick of the plague in the hospital and district together, and it was spreading to the camp also."

The plague was carried by rats who had been disturbed by the rampaging armies. The disease was communicated to humans by fleas. Its symptoms were swellings in the armpits and groin. More than half of those who became infected by the plague died of it, their bodies marked by many small, dark hemorrhage spots. Death came after three horrible and terrifying days. Nothing could prevent it. It was thought that the plague was carried by the air, and if only the air were made to stir into a breeze and cleanse itself, the plague would pass. Thus guns were fired, bells rung, cacophonous, mournful music was played, and the rich fled to their country villas. Gravediggers, drawn from the ranks of condemned prisoners, would cart the bodies off to communal graves, becoming, as they did so, especially dreadful bogeymen.

Meanwhile, in the realm of grand strategy, Federigo da Montefeltro continued his siege of Sansovino. Ercole d'Este moved the Florentine troops smartly down into the Chiana Valley, and then pitched camp at a safe distance from Federigo's forces. Sansovino capitulated in the face of Federigo's siege, and—November having come—the customary winter truce was called and the armies returned to their winter quarters. "And during these days," Landucci recorded, "the Arno was very high and overflowed its

banks. . . . It caused great damage. . . . And the plague was also causing much mortality. . . . And at this Christmas-time, what with terror of the war, the plague, and the papal excommunication, the citizens were in sorry plight. They lived in dread. . . ."

Renaissance warfare did not often owe much to bravery. Wars were rather wars of attrition. Much has been said about rampaging mercenaries who plundered and devastated farm lands and towns during the Renaissance, as though this indicated some lack of discipline among the troops. In fact, however, the principal strategy of war was systematic plunder. Armies were expected, first of all, to provision themselves in enemy territory by looting and to employ theft as a means of acquiring bonuses. Then they were meant, too, to behave as an organized plague, destroying crops, seizing goods and money, spreading poverty, fear, famine, and economic chaos.

When an army laid siege to a town, the condottieri first offered to accept a cash tribute from the town. Failing a tribute, the army would negotiate for a conditional surrender, which would provide that the inhabitants of the town could leave with whatever they could carry before their town was sacked. Failing even this, a town could

A new outbreak of the plague was an ever-present possibility. Above, a merry party of hunters comes upon the coffins of three victims of the plague, and a monk (upper left) reminds them of the transitoriness of human pleasures.

surrender and depend on the mercy of the enemy, the assumption being that the troops would do less damage if they did not have to injure themselves by storming the town. Sometimes a town would agree to surrender by a certain date if no relief force came to their rescue—such as Ercole d'Este's relief force.

If a town refused to surrender, it was laid under siege, and the besieging troops became hungrier, and doubtless angrier, the longer the siege lasted. If, finally, the army broke through the town walls after a battle in which injuries and deaths and equipment losses were heavy, the town might be taken apart in an orgy of greed and rage. Houses would be demolished, women raped, men murdered.

The worst and bloodiest battles occurred when a besieging army actually was attacked by a force sent to relieve a town. Then the besiegers, under threat of losing the booty for which they had been waiting, threw themselves furiously into battle. Cavalries would charge one another, infantry soldiers would fight hand to hand with swords and shields, and hundreds of bodies might be left on the field. It was doubtless for this reason that Ercole d'Este kept his distance from Sansovino in 1478.

Camp life was evidently not too boring for these armies who circled continuously about one another. Italian armies were noted for their large followings of women. The soldiers gambled, drank good wine, tended to repairs on arms and armor, and, if there were recent spoils in the camp, often engaged in bloody fights among themselves over the booty.

In the spring of 1479 the Pazzi War resumed. After another season of marches, countermarches, sieges, and retreats, ending in stalemate, Lorenzo de' Medici left Florence for Naples, where he sued for peace. The treaty he concluded was not entirely satisfactory, and did not definitely end the war. The Venetians did not care for the agreement. They made an alliance with the pope, and disputes and occasional military maneuvers, leading to the War of Ferrara, continued until 1484. When peace was eventually concluded, Pope Sixtus IV died. "Nothing could daunt the fierce Sixtus," according to a saying that went around Italy, "yet, when he heard the word peace, he died."

The Pazzi War was a pluperfect Renaissance war, rooted in family rivalries, waged by mercenaries, careful of the lives of professional soldiers, wasteful of the civilian population and their property, productive of famine, plague, rape, and murder, and drawn to an inconclusive ending that displeased all the participants and left unsolved disputes to be made into causes of war another day. The condottieri returned to their permanent quarters to review their losses, which were reckoned in terms not of lives lost but of equipment that needed to be replaced. Citizens of the many small towns that had been sacked set about restoring town walls and houses. Vineyards had to be replanted. Florence was deeply in debt, its treasury in a shambles. Odd bands of mercenaries that had broken away from the armies continued to roam about the countryside, terrorizing farmers, robbing merchants, murdering travelers, spreading fear, lawlessness, chaos.

To be sure, other Renaissance wars did yield opportunities for splendid pitched battles. In one such struggle, two generations before the Pazzi War, the Florentine captain general, Niccoló da Tolentino, met an army of Sienese and Milanese troops in the Arno Valley. With the help of another force under Micheletto Attendolo, he pursued the enemy into an open plain. Niccoló attacked abruptly on one flank, Micheletto on another, and they utterly destroyed the Sienese, taking prisoner a number of enemy condottieri, one hundred and fifty soldiers, and six hundred horses. The battle was known as the Rout of San Romano, and it was so superbly executed that it was immortalized in a set of wonderful paintings of rearing horses, beplumed helmeted knights with lances, battle-axes, trumpets, and banners, charging and hacking at one another in a thrilling riot of death and bright colors. The paintings, by Paolo Uccello, decorated the bedroom of Lorenzo de' Medici when he was a boy. In all his adult years, Lorenzo would never know a war that was quite so much fun. In truth, this battle—like the condottiere celebrated in Verrocchio's equestrian statue, like the civilized military man Federigo da Montefeltro—was painted precisely because it was of a sort so exceedingly rare.

The Italians of the Renaissance are, in the end, strikingly reminiscent of the modern Mafia—warm-spirited, generous, religious, given to robust singing, sentimental, and capable of quick, stunning, brutal violence. They preyed largely on the powerless and the poor, they fought among themselves, and they could never quite overcome family loyalties, jealousies, and personal drives for wealth and power to join together in a united country.

Toward the end of the fifteenth century, as Italian merchant-bankers came to be on familiar terms with foreign courts, Italian rulers of city-states would call upon France or Spain to send troops into Italy to join a war. The French came in 1494, and twice more. Then came the Germans and the Spanish. From these invasions, Italy never recovered, and never learned.

Condottieri, professional men-at-arms who sold their services to the highest bidder, played a vital part in Italy's wars. The condottiere opposite, Bartolommeo Colleoni, led Venetian forces—and died old, rich, and full of honors.

51

CHAPTER V

THE COURTIER

The very violence and brutality of the Renaissance produced an urgent need for civility and for mutual respect. If private family ambitions would never be sacrificed to an overreaching public good, if economic and political rivalry presented intractable problems, at least the men and women of the Renaissance could try to be polite in their daily lives. When they were not at one another's throats, they went to remarkable lengths to be agreeable.

At the end of their wars, the more favored Italian condottieri returned not to rude billets but, often, to their own comfortable courts — Ercole d'Este to Ferrara, Roberto Malatesta to Rimini, Federigo da Montefeltro to Urbino — to repair their arms and cultivate their souls. Away from the battlefield, Federigo, who sits uncomfortably in full armor on the opposite page, ruled his city-state with absolute, although benevolent, power. Republics came, and were corrupted, in Florence and Siena and Pisa and other smaller towns. Oligarchies ruled in many places. But the Montefeltro family owned its own state and ruled without any check on their powers. In this they resembled the Estes, who ruled Ferrara from the thirteenth to the late sixteenth century, and the Gonzagas, who ruled Mantua from the fourteenth

A condottiere who became duke of Urbino, Federigo da Montefeltro, opposite with son Guidobaldo, was also a scholar and art patron — and a model for the young noblemen who gathered at his court, such as the ones in the inset above.

century to the early eighteenth.

They gained and maintained their states, most of these families, as old feudal lords had once done, by fighting for pope or king, or such large city-states as Venice and Milan and Florence. They had originally conquered, or been given, their fiefs, or wrested them from the control of republican governments, and, with time, they had increased their power and wealth and independence. At the time of the Renaissance, they constituted Italy's aristocracy and were the models for much emulation, even though, as is often the case with aristocrats, they sometimes had neither as much wealth nor power as the newer families.

Federigo, in fact, enjoyed a prosperous domain. It was said of his palace that "it seemed not a palace but a city in the form of a palace; and [Federigo] furnished it not only with what is customary, such as silver vases, wall-hangings of the richest cloth of gold, silk, and other like things, but for ornament he added countless ancient statues of marble and bronze . . . and musical instruments of every sort; nor did he wish to have anything there that was not most rare and excellent. . . ." He had a staff of two hundred servants, thirty or forty of whom spent all their time copying books (Federigo would not deign to have cheap printed books), and his library was famous throughout Europe as one of the largest, and most expensive, of the time.

At Ferrara, the Estes commissioned paintings

from Mantegna, Pisanello, and Francesco del Cossa, and gathered about them many of the interesting writers of the time. Matteo Maria Boiardo wrote his epic poem of Arthurian chivalry and love, *Orlando Innamorato*, at Ferrara. Lodovico Ariosto wrote *Orlando Furioso*, a brilliant fantasy, both romantic and satirical, that is generally accounted the best epic poem of the time. Ancient Latin comedies were translated and staged, and playwrights abounded—among them Giovanni Battista Giraldi, who is chiefly remembered because Shakespeare borrowed from Giraldi's plots for his own Italian plays.

At Mantua, Alberti was employed to design new buildings, Mantegna decorated a room with some of the finest frescoes of the fifteenth century, Greek scholars and playwrights were kept about the court, Angelo Poliziano wrote his play *Orfeo*. The smart set of writers, artists, intellectuals, poets, young cardinals, and courtiers passed through Mantua to pause for a few days or years, to meet one another, to talk, to trade ideas and witticisms and gossip which they spread on their travels to other courts.

One Mantuan, Baldassare Castiglione, moved on to live at the court of Urbino, which, by that time, was ruled by Federigo's son Guidobaldo and his wife Elisabetta, a Gonzaga from Mantua. According to Castiglione, who wrote of the life at Urbino in his *Book of the Courtier*, it was "the custom of all the gentlemen of the house to betake themselves immediately after supper to the Duchess [Elisabetta]; where, amidst the pleasant pastimes, the music and dancing which were continually enjoyed, fine questions would sometimes be proposed, and sometimes ingenious games. . . ."

Among the guests at Urbino in Castiglione's time were Bernardo Accolti, famous as a quick-witted improviser of verse; Giuliano de' Medici, the youngest son of Lorenzo; Bernardo Bibbiena, an author of comedies and later a cardinal; Pietro Bembo, a Venetian noble, an authority on language, and later a cardinal; Ottaviano Fregoso,

---

Baldassare Castiglione (above left), who lived at Urbino in the court of Federigo's son, Duke Guidobaldo, personified the ideal of knightly behavior he set forth in his influential book, **The Courtier.** *In its English version (left) it was much consulted by Elizabethan gentlemen.*

a Genoese noble and later doge of Genoa; Count Lodovico da Canossa of Verona, later a bishop and ambassador; and many others. They gathered in a large, handsome room around a fireplace, with Elisabetta and her friend Emilia Pia, a widow, at the center of the circle, and, in the conversational game reconstructed by Castiglione, they defined the ideal courtier—a definition that has persisted for five centuries as the prototype of the perfect gentleman.

"I would have our Courtier born of a noble and genteel family," said the noble and genteel Count da Canossa, ". . . for noble birth is like a bright lamp that makes manifest and visible deeds both good and bad. . . . And since this luster of nobility does not shine forth in the deeds of the lowly born, they lack that spur, as well as that fear of dishonor. . . ." Then, too, said the count, he would have the Courtier "endowed by nature not only with talent and with beauty of countenance and person, but with that certain grace we call an 'air.' . . ."

Gasparo Pallavicino demurred: ". . . to me this nobility of birth does not seem so essential. . . . I would adduce many instances of persons born of the noblest blood who have been ridden by vices; and, on the contrary, many persons of humble birth who, through their virtue, have made their posterity illustrious."

The count: "I do not deny that the same virtues can rule in the lowborn as in the wellborn: but . . . since it is our task to form a Courtier free of any defect whatsoever, and endowed with all that is praise-worthy, I deem it necessary to have him be of noble birth."

The count would also have the perfect Courtier be handsome—not delicate, but manly "and yet full of grace"—neither too big nor too small, possessed of "strength and lightness and suppleness." His first duty would be "to know how to handle every kind of weapon," and "be especially acquainted with those arms that are ordinarily used among gentlemen." He should know how to swim, jump, run, throw stones, play tennis, and be a perfect horseman. He should be able "to tilt and joust. . . . In tourneys, in holding a pass, in attacking a fortified position, let him be among the best of the French. In stick-throwing, bull-fighting, in casting spears and darts, let him be outstanding among the Spaniards. But, above all, let him temper his every action with a certain good judgment and grace . . . let him laugh, jest, banter, frolic, and dance, yet in such a manner as to show always that he is genial and discreet; and let him be full of grace in all that he does or says." The ideal Courtier should exhibit a certain *sprezzatura*, or nonchalance, "so as to conceal all art and make whatever is done or said appear to be without effort and almost without any thought about it."

The Courtier was to be a performer, too: "Whenever the Courtier chances to be engaged in a skirmish . . . or a battle in the field . . . he should discreetly withdraw from the crowd, and do the outstanding and daring things that he has to do in as small a company as possible and in the sight of all the noblest and most respected men in the army. . . . Whereas, if he happens to engage in arms in some public show—such as jousts, tourneys, stick-throwing, or in any other bodily exercise . . . he will strive to be as elegant and handsome in the exercise of arms as he is adroit, and to feed his spectators' eyes with all those things that he thinks may give him added grace. . . ."

As others joined the conversation, other prescriptions were added on how the Courtier must speak and write, and be able to play a musical instrument, how he must be acquainted with painting and be able himself to draw. Such topics as these gave the assembled company an opportunity to bring out other set-pieces of polite Renaissance conversation, such as whether painting or sculpture is the superior art form.

While it is true that Castiglione is writing about an ideal in his *Book of the Courtier,* there can be no doubt that many of his contemporaries measured up to his standards, or tried to measure up. The conversations flow naturally and easily: it was a society that talked of philosophy and music and art, and sprinkled its talk with references to Raphael and Michelangelo, Ovid and Livy. The conversations have wit and candor, too; a less nobly born participant does not hesitate to twit Canossa about his snobbishness. And one has only to look at Renaissance portraits to see that an air of gravity and elegance, nonchalance and self-assurance, was cultivated. And yet, it is only in impolite societies that rules of politeness have to be talked about at such length.

None of the participants in Castiglione's Platonic dialogue can have been unaware of the fact that their court was supported by the proceeds of messily ignoble wars. In the way they went about creating a style of heightened civility, they shared with their contemporaries a sort of heady contrariness: in a time of transition, when no individual could control the destiny of the world, Renaissance men promulgated the notion of a human-centered universe with man firmly in control; in a time of unfathomable events, philosophers laid the foundations of modern Western rationalism; in a time of repressive government, humanists praised individual freedom; and in a time of brutal violence and surpassing vulgarity, the group at Urbino defined a "gentleman." The Renaissance was, above all, the era of the *tour de force*.

"I would have him more than passably learned in letters," the count said, "at least in those studies which we call the humanities. Let him be conversant not only with the Latin language, but with Greek as well, because of the abundance and variety of things that are so divinely written therein. Let him be versed in the poets, as well as in the orators and historians, and let him be practiced also in writing verse and prose, especially in our own vernacular. . . .

"These studies . . . will make him fluent, and (as Aristippus said to the tyrant) bold and self-confident in speaking with everyone. However, I would have our Courtier keep one precept firmly in mind, namely in this as in everything else, to be cautious and reserved rather than forward. . . ."

In conversation, added Federico Fregoso, brother of Ottaviano and nephew of Duke Guidobaldo, the Courtier "must perceive the differences between one man and another, and change his style and method from day to day, according to the nature of the person with whom he undertakes to converse." As for dancing, "I think he should maintain a certain dignity, though tempered with a fine and airy grace of movement; and . . . let him not attempt those quick movements of foot and those double steps . . . which would perhaps little befit a gentleman. . . ."

In music, "the most beautiful music is in singing well and in reading at sight and in fine style, but even more in singing to the accompaniment

This villa, which Lorenzo de' Medici had built for him at Poggio a Caiano, was apparently not intended as a country retreat, but as a center for study by the leading scholars of the world.

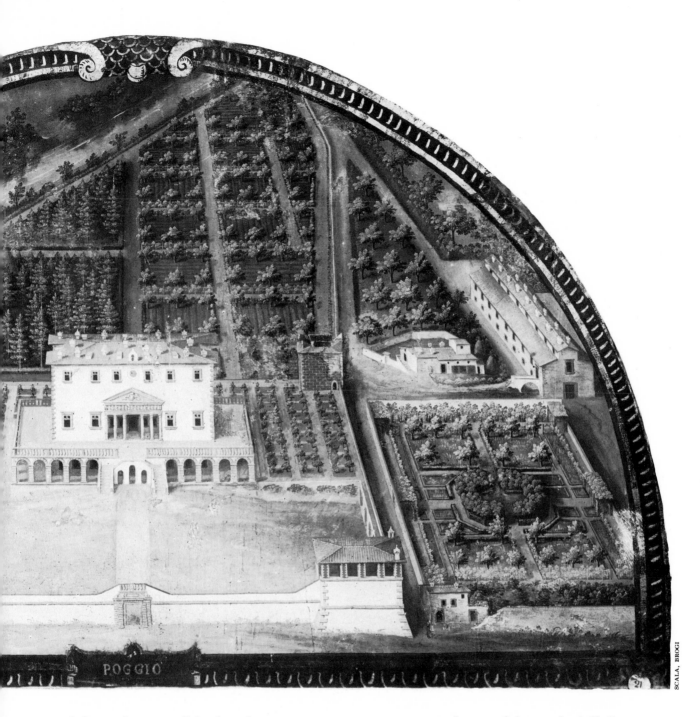

POGGIO

of the viola. . . . All keyboard instruments are harmonious because their consonances are most perfect, and they lend themselves to the performance of many things that fill the soul with musical sweetness. And no less delightful is the music of four violas which is most suave and exquisite. . . ."

From time to time, the conversations at Urbino were interrupted for music or dancing. Sometimes they continued through the night until dawn, when, in the summertime, with the windows open, "a soft breeze seemed to come that filled the air with a brisk coolness and began to awaken sweet concerts of joyous birds in the murmuring forests of the nearby hills."

The proper dress for the Courtier, it was said, should "not be extreme in any way, as the French are sometimes in being over-ample, and the Germans in being over-scanty. . . . I prefer [clothes] always to tend a little more toward the grave and sober rather than the foppish. Hence, I think that black is more pleasing in clothing than any other color; and if not black, then at least some color on the dark side. I mean this of ordinary attire, for there is no doubt that . . . it is also more appropriate for gala dress to be trimmed, showy, and dashing. . . ." Multicolored hose and particolored doublets were coming into

57

Music was an indispensable part of Renaissance life, and many a nobleman kept musicians like the ones above on his staff, to play and sing at banquets, balls, shows, and other occasions.

fashion, and the young Federico Fregoso declared: "Who of us, on seeing a gentleman pass by dressed in a habit quartered in varied colors, or with an array of strings and ribbons and bows and cross-lacings, does not take him to be a fool or a buffoon?"

The gentlemen of Urbino did not omit a single particular in describing the perfect Courtier, even to the extent of specifying the proper games for a gentleman to play: This part of the conversation permitted Federico to score a nice point. As for chess, he said, "it seems to me to have one defect, which is that it is possible to have too much knowledge of it, so that whoever would excel in the game must give a great deal of time to it, as I believe, and as much study as if he would learn some noble science . . . and yet in the end, for all his pains, he only knows how to play a game. Thus, I think a very unusual thing happens in this, namely, that mediocrity is more to be praised than excellence."

Bernardo Bibbiena was given the task of defining the ideal courtly sense of humor: "if the Courtier, with his banter and witticisms, has regard for time, person, and his own rank, and takes care not to use them too often . . . he may be called a humorous man; providing if he takes care also not to be so sharp and biting that he be known as malicious and as one who attacks without cause or with evident rancor either those who are very powerful, which is imprudent, or those who are too weak, which is cruel, or those who are too wicked, which is useless, or says things that offend persons whom he would not wish to offend, which is ignorance."

With those general guidelines in mind, Bibbiena proceeded to regale the court with dozens and dozens of jokes, anecdotes, instances of pleasantries, puns, ripostes, and every variety of Renaissance humor. Once, the future cardinal said, when he asked someone why it was "that on Good Friday, when the Church prayed not only for Christians but even for pagans and Jews, no mention was made of cardinals along with bishops and other prelates, he answered me that cardinals were intended in the prayer that says: 'Let us pray for heretics and schismatics.'"

Bibbiena remembered a debate in the Florentine Signoria when a member of the Altoviti family fell asleep. The man next to him roused him, saying, "Do you not hear what that man is saying? Make answer, as the Signors are asking for your opinion." Thinking one of his rivals of the Alamanni family must have been speaking, Altoviti rose and said, "Gentlemen, I say just the opposite of what Alamanni said." Alamanni replied: "Oh, but I have said nothing." Without a moment's hesitation Altoviti declared: "Then the opposite of what you will say."

Many of these jokes do not travel well through the centuries. One is a superb example of what seemed funny before the age of paper money: when a city ran short of funds to prosecute a war, a citizen suggested in Council "that the mints . . . be set running . . . and that they do nothing day and night but mint money, and let it all be gold ducats. . . ." This was supposed to be a humorous absurdity.

The ultimate duty of this polished, urbane, knowledgeable, well-born, witty Courtier was very simply to serve his prince. As Duke Guidobaldo's nephew Federico said, "I would have the Courtier devote all his thought and strength of spirit to loving and almost adoring the prince he serves above all else, devoting his every desire and habit and manner to pleasing him."

Some of Federico's worldly-wise elders attempted to cool his youthful ardor. They spoke of the need to resist tyranny, of the duty of the Courtier to inform and help educate the prince, and so forth. For the most part, however, they agreed that service to the prince was their principal duty. Of course, perfect Courtiers gave perfect service only to perfect princes, and the ideal prince embraced a love of justice, of his country and his people; he was prudent, good, humane;

The passion for gambling that swept Italy in the fifteenth century ruined so many great Venetian families that the Council of Ten prohibited the sale of dice and cards. A more respectable pastime was a game of chess (above).

and, to make a perfectly harmonious hierarchy of the whole system, the prince ultimately owed his service to God.

Indeed, the essential problem in Castiglione's perfect modern gentleman is that he is all style, all form, and no substance. He had no beliefs, no burning convictions, no goal of his own except perfect worldliness. The essential hollowness of the Courtier, his need to find his *raison d' être*, like his divertissements, in externals, left him peculiarly vulnerable.

Not all princes achieved the informed benevolence of the Montefeltros and Estes and Gonzagas. Urbino's neighboring state of Rimini was ruled by the Malatestas. Sigismondo, who died in 1468, was equally famous as a patron of poets and scholars, as the man who commissioned Alberti to design the Malatesta temple, and as the violent husband of Ginevra d'Este, who mysteriously "died" after five years of marriage, and

59

of Polissena Sforza of Milan, who "died" after seven years of marriage. Sigismondo's son Roberto carried on the Malatesta tradition of violence, without his father's interest in arts and letters, and Rimini was wracked by family feud, riot, war, and disaster. Cesare Borgia took the town; Pandolfo Malatesta, amid the struggles, sacked his own town; Rimini was finally simply sold to Venice. The Malatesta temple remains unfinished.

If Castiglione recorded the sometimes achieved goals of princes, the man who recorded the cynical underlying reality of their rule was Niccolò Machiavelli in his book *The Prince*. Machiavelli wrote the book as a bit of unsolicited advice to the Medicis. In the late fifteenth century, the Medicis had been expelled from Florence, and they devoted most of their efforts, which were ultimately successful, to finding ways to reestablish themselves in Florence — this time as openly acknowledged princely rulers, like the Estes and Montefeltros. In drafting his treatise on how to gain such rule, Machiavelli drew on the careers of Cesare Borgia and of the Sforzas of Milan for examples of effective political maneuvers, and yet he had in mind other princely precedents in drawing up his strictures. In sum, his rules, like Castiglione's, tell us something of the day-to-day life of princes and their courts.

How we live, Machiavelli said, "is so far removed from how we ought to live, that he who abandons what is done for what ought to be done, will rather learn to bring about his own ruin than his preservation. A man who wishes to make a profession of goodness in everything must necessarily come to grief among so many who are not good. Therefore it is necessary for a prince, who wishes to maintain himself, to learn how not to be good, and to use this knowledge and not use it, according to the necessity of the case."

In these terms, Machiavelli advised, "it would be well to be considered liberal" but not to be so, since liberality is expensive, and "there is nothing which destroys itself so much as liberality, for by using it you lose the power of using it. . . ." Furthermore, a prince "must not mind incurring the charge of cruelty for the purpose of keeping his subjects united and faithful . . . it is much safer to be feared than loved . . . the experience of our times shows those princes to

Incumbent on the prince was the duty to foster art and learning. Above, Ercole d'Este, patron of the epic poet Lodovico Ariosto and the father of Isabella and Beatrice d'Este, receives a new book from its kneeling author, a monk.

have done great things who have had little regard for good faith . . . as [men] are bad, and would not observe their faith with you, so you are not bound to keep faith with them. . . ."

A prince should be *seen*, Machiavelli said, as "merciful, faithful, humane, sincere, religious, and also . . . be so; but you must have the mind so disposed that when it is needful to be otherwise you may be able to change to the opposite qualities. And . . . be able to do evil if constrained." Princes will not be despised for this hypocrisy, because "the vulgar crowd is always taken in by appearances and the issue of the event; and the world consists only of the vulgar, and the few who are not vulgar are isolated when the many have a rallying point in the prince."

Finally, Machiavelli advised, a prince should "show himself a lover of merit, give preferment to the able, and honor those who excel in every art. . . . Besides this, he ought, at convenient seasons of the year, to keep the people occupied with festivals and shows. . . ." All of these devices were to be employed to get and keep power. Machiavelli had despaired of the idea that rulers should have any higher goal.

Against Machiavelli's prince, Castiglione's Courtier simply had no defense. In times of good leaders, he was the perfect establishmentarian; unfortunately, in times of bad leaders, he was still the perfect establishmentarian. Thus, as in chess, so in gentlemanliness, it may be that perfection is less to be praised than mediocrity.

61

This courtier was presumably good at archery—and at horsemanship, fencing, and other knightly arts.

CHAPTER VI

THE RENAISSANCE WOMAN

The gentlemen of Urbino no sooner finished describing the perfect gentleman than one of their number, whom delicacy forbids naming, did a most ungentlemanly thing: he insulted womanhood, saying that women "are very imperfect creatures." The assembled company turned on the villain, and, after some minor conversational skirmishing, agreed to fashion a Court Lady who would be an appropriate counterpart to the Courtier. The man appointed by the Duchess Elisabetta to make the opening statement was Giuliano de' Medici, the youngest son of Lorenzo.

"I think," said Giuliano, "that in her ways, manners, words, gestures, and bearing, a woman ought to be very unlike a man. . . . It is seemly for a woman to have a soft and delicate tenderness, with an air of womanly sweetness in her every movement. . . . Now, if this precept be added to the rules which these gentlemen have taught the Courtier, then I think she ought to be able to follow many such and adorn herself with the best accomplishments." A Lady, said Giuliano, should have all those characteristics of prudence, magnanimity, continence, kindness, and discretion suited to a Courtier and, if she is

MUSÉE DE CLUNY, PARIS

married, "ability to manage her husband's property and house and children . . . and all qualities that are requisite in a good mother. . . ." Then, too, "in a Lady who lives at court a certain pleasing affability is becoming above all else, whereby she will be able to entertain graciously every kind of man with agreeable and comely conversation suited to the time and place and to the station of the person with whom she speaks."

Lest these general remarks not provide sufficient guidelines, Giuliano elaborated: "The Court Lady must have not only the good judgment to recognize the kind of person with whom she is speaking, but must have knowledge of many things, in order to entertain that person graciously; and let her know how in her talk to choose those things that are suited to the kind of person with whom she is speaking, and be careful lest, unintentionally, she might sometimes utter words that could offend him. . . . In this way she will be adorned with good manners; she will perform with surpassing grace the bodily exercises that are proper to women; her discourse will be fluent and most prudent, virtuous, and pleasant; thus, she will be not only loved but revered by everyone, and perhaps worthy of being considered the equal of this great Courtier, both in qualities of mind and of body."

It is easy to see how a Court Lady could degenerate into a courtesan, and the cultivated

The young lady opposite, attended by servants, seems to personify Giuliano de' Medici's feminine ideal, "with an air of womanly sweetness in her every movement." In the muddy streets, she might wear platform sandals (inset above).

63

Unlike her sister Beatrice, who died young, Isabella d'Este (above) led a long life, which, while not a happy one, nevertheless gave ample scope to her intelligence—and her gifts for manipulating the destinies of men and states.

courtesan flourished, especially in Venice and Rome. The most famous among them were known for their sumptuous houses; they rode about in fine coaches, discoursed easily of Cicero and Ovid and Petrarch, sang, danced, played the lute, and behaved generally like well-born court ladies. As the Courtier was intended to serve his prince, so the Court Lady was intended to serve men. The perfect woman was defined by men—the Duchess Elisabetta continued to preside over the conversation and mostly remain silent—and the perfect woman was declared free and equal, but, of course, she was not. Nor indeed were the men who defined the Court Lady as free as they liked to think they were. All were bound to a hierarchical structure, a lingering social, if not economic, feudalism that was remarkably confining. The

men and women of the Renaissance broke many of their old bonds, but not all, and not all at once. As new Renaissance ideals of freedom were laid over old feudal usages, tensions and self-contradictions were inevitable. And if men were able to seize upon liberating Renaissance ideas, they often kept women bound by older conventions— and could do so as long as they remained the definers.

Yet, for all these objections, it is true that the gentlemen of Urbino defined a woman who was far more independent and far more able to shape her own fate than the female chattels of the Middle Ages, or even than the ordinary woman of Florence, who was to be treated like a spirited and recalcitrant horse. What seems in retrospect tame was at the time revolutionary; and the men of the Renaissance did, in fact, set forth a notion of women that persisted as the Western ideal right up to our own day.

Not all of Castiglione's courtiers liked what they heard about these new women. Signor Gasparo inquired acidly of Giuliano what exercises might be appropriate to a Court Lady, and whether all the virtues "you have named are supposed to help her merely in the management of her house, children, and family (which, however, you do not wish to be her principal profession), or rather in her conversation and graceful practice of these bodily exercises; and, by your faith, take care not to set these virtues to such menial tasks that they will be ashamed."

"I think," said Giuliano, "there is none here who does not recognize that, as for bodily exercises, it is not seemly for a woman to handle weapons, ride, play tennis, wrestle, and do many other things that are suited to men."

The improviser of verse, Accolti, chimed in: "With the ancients it was the custom for women to wrestle naked with men, but we have lost that good practice, along with many others."

One of the younger members of the Gonzaga family, Cesare, added: "And in my time, I have seen women play tennis, handle weapons, ride, hunt, and engage in nearly all the exercises that a cavalier can."

"Since I may fashion this Lady as I please," Giuliano replied, "not only would I not have her engage in such robust and strenuous manly exercises, but even those that are becoming to a woman I would have her practice in a measured way and with that gentle delicacy that we have said befits her. . . ." In singing, Giuliano would have her sing softly and sweetly; in dancing, he would not have his Lady move too energetically; nor would he have her play drums, fifes, trumpets, "or other like instruments."

As for her intellectual attainments, Giuliano would have his Lady know "that which these gentlemen wished the Courtier to know," including "a knowledge of letters, of music, of painting and . . . how to be festive, adding a discreet modesty and the giving of a good impression of herself to those other things that have been required of the Courtier."

Signor Gasparo returned to the attack: "I am quite surprised that you do not wish them to govern cities, make laws, lead armies and let the men stay at home to cook or spin."

To Gasparo's astonishment, while Giuliano neglected to commend cooking and spinning for men, he replied, "Perhaps that would not be so bad either. . . . Don't you know that Plato, who certainly was no great friend to women, put them in charge of the city and gave all martial duties to the men? Don't you believe that many women could be found who would know how to govern cities and armies as well as men do?" He had not given them these duties, Giuliano said, only because he was "fashioning a Court Lady, not a Queen."

Gasparo attacked from another angle, saying that "learned men have written that, since nature always intends and plans to make things most perfect, she would constantly bring forth men if she could; and that when a woman is born, it is a defect or mistake of nature . . . as is seen too in the case of one who is born blind, or lame, or with some other defect. . . . Thus, a woman can be said to be a creature produced by chance and accident."

Giuliano replied with a Platonic argument concerning "essences" and "accidents," and concluded: "I say that women can understand all the things men can understand and that the intellect of a woman can penetrate wherever a man's can."

Gasparo, slipping into a defensive last stand, declared that "all women without exception desire to be men, by a certain natural instinct

Notwithstanding her angelic appearance in the portrait above, Lucrezia Borgia left a name synonymous with treachery, though she was outdone in villainousness by her father, the simoniac Pope Alexander VI, and her evil brother Cesare.

that teaches them to desire their own perfection."

Giuliano: "The poor creatures do not desire to be men in order to become more perfect, but in order to gain freedom and to escape that rule over them which man has arrogated to himself by his own authority."

As for questions of love, Giuliano said, "I think she ought to be governed by nobody's wish but her own." The young Federico Gonzaga went so far as to say that even once women were married they ought to be free to love whomever they wished. "If women were allowed," he said, "to get a divorce and separate from those with whom they are ill-mated, then perhaps they would be without excuse if they loved any man except their husband; but when they are ill-starred or ill-suited by temperament or for

*In the fields outside Florence, the sight of peas-
ant women picking spinach was a familiar one.*

some other reason," they ought to be free to have
any lovers they please.

Giuliano stopped short of such extreme license, however: "They wrong themselves by
loving any man except their husband. Still, since
it is often times not in our power to refuse to love,
if this mishap should befall a Court Lady . . . I
would have her give her lover a spiritual love
only. . . ."

As for an unmarried woman, "I wish her to love
someone whom she can marry; nor will I reckon
it a fault if she gives him some sign of love. . . ."
But, "let her show her lover every sign of love
except such as may give him hope of obtaining
something dishonorable from her."

Another of the men objected that Giuliano had
made the Court Lady "a little too austere"; but
Giuliano replied that "if the Courtier be as courteous and discreet as these gentlemen have made
him, he will not only not hope for, but will not
even desire" anything dishonorable from a
Court Lady.

We must wonder whether in this Giuliano was
gently deflating the pretensions built up for
the Courtier. The image that Castiglione's in-
terlocutors made of a perfect gentleman and a
perfect lady, both attractive, talented, well-
educated, physically active, and free to make
sexual choices—but bound to avoid anything
"dishonorable"—is a prescription for frustra-
tion, also known as courtly love. The idea of
courtly love—a woman on a pedestal, flirtatious
but demure, adored by a man who performs for
her in tournaments, conversation, poems, and
other chivalric services—was presumed to
furnish men and women with a constant, exquisite torture, giving their lives a safe piquancy,
and lending society a set of tantalizing worldly
rituals far more complex than anything the
Church ever had to offer. The men and women
of the Renaissance imagined that this was Platonic love, and they seem to have enjoyed it as
much for its classical *frisson* as for anything else.

Most memoirs and diaries remain resolutely
discreet about sexual affairs during the Renaissance, but the frescoes that decorate the walls
of Ferrara's Schifanoia Palace (see pages 68-69)
may be more revealing. There, it would seem,
poetry and music and flirtation have led to the
predictable conclusion of kissing and caressing—
two unmentionable topics in the *Book of the
Courtier;* and we have no reason to imagine that,
having so far violated Giuliano de' Medici's code
of behavior, the courtiers and their ladies felt
constrained by the code at all. The extraordinary number of rabbits in the painting do not
betoken an interest in zoology.

For all the qualifications that must be placed
around any Renaissance claims to new freedoms,
new humanistic philosophies, new enjoyment of
a human-centered, world-conscious universe,
the spirit of striving to achieve full human potential and autonomy is one of the prime characteristics of the Renaissance. This explosive spirit
was probably accompanied by a far more open
attitude toward sex—if, indeed, it was not caused
by new sexual attitudes.

Still, said Signor Gasparo, "I do not see . . .
how you can deny that man is by his natural qualities more perfect than woman." He did not
think Giuliano could name many great women.

But, of course, Giuliano could, beginning with

66

Eyes on the ball, a noblewoman prepares to swing her bat. The game, the giuoco della palla, was a precursor of tennis.

classical Romans: "If you examine ancient histories (although men have always been very chary in writing praise of women) and modern histories, you will find that worth has constantly prevailed among women as among men. . . . Then, if you would speak of present times, we shall not need to look far afield for examples, because we have them here before us."

And, aside from the Duchess Elisabetta, Giuliano mentioned among many others Queen Isabella of Spain, Eleanora of Aragon, Isabella of Aragon, Beatrice d'Este, and Isabella d'Este, marchioness of Mantua.

The fact that the conversations recorded in

the *Book of the Courtier* occurred at the court of Urbino can perhaps be explained by a bit of gossip. Elisabetta's husband Guidobaldo had been the victim of all sorts of minor illnesses beginning in his teens. Married to Elisabetta at the age of sixteen, Guidobaldo discovered that he was suddenly, and ever after, impotent. The

The idyllic scene below, an allegorical representation of April painted around 1470, shows how greatly the spirit of humanism had by then triumphed over the strictures of the medieval Church. At center, Venus, pulled along by swans, is being wooed by Mars, her love slave in chains, while elsewhere youths and maidens engage in amorous play, oblivious of the rabbits, folk symbols of sexuality and fertility.

In the relatively rare event of heavy snow, the ladies joined their lords in snow fights. Exercise, said the versatile Leon Battista Alberti, himself no mean sportsman, was necessary for young people and useful for the old—of both sexes.

psychodynamics of this impotence are beyond knowing, but the ensuing history of the court is not. Guidobaldo and Elisabetta had both read their Dante and Petrarch, and absorbed a good deal of neo-Platonism, and their marriage was characterized by a sort of lofty mutual devotion. In 1502, when Guidobaldo was thirty years old, he ran afoul of the Borgia Pope Alexander VI's dynastic ambitions. The pope's son Cesare Borgia took Urbino, Guidobaldo and Elisabetta were driven out, and Alexander VI offered Elisabetta an annulment of her marriage—and a vigorous French husband—which she refused. The Montefeltros were later restored to Urbino, and Elisabetta spent her last eight years as a widow, with Castiglione living at her court. There is no reason to believe that she and Castiglione had anything other than a proper courtly relationship.

If the gossip explains the need for courtly love in Urbino, it does not explain how the phenomenon, and the image of the modern lady and gentleman, swept Europe. We can only conclude that the new near-equality of men and women was an extraordinarily liberating phenomenon for both sexes. Of all the women to emerge in this new atmosphere, one of the most characteristic in both freedoms and limitations, and most widely admired, was Elisabetta's close friend and sister-in-law, Isabella d'Este.

Born in 1474 in Ferrara, Isabella was given the same classical education that any well-born boy would have had. She danced, with "grace and elegance" according to princess-watchers, by the age of five, and later showed a particular talent for music, playing both the lute and clavichord, and she had a beautiful singing voice. By the age of fourteen, she was singing lines from Petrarch and Virgil that had been set to music for her. Her father, who was enamored of the classical authors, especially Plutarch, Euripides, and Seneca, had the comedies of Plautus and Terence translated into Italian and staged at the court of Ferrara. Her mother was something of a connoisseur of painting, and Isabella's childhood was spent among frescoes by Pisanello, Piero della Francesca, and Francesco Cossa. When she grew up, Isabella would be known for speaking Latin better than any woman of her age (no men are mentioned in the comparison), and for being one of the most discerning and demanding patrons, of either sex, of painters of the Renaissance.

She was married in 1490, for political, not romantic reasons, to Francesco Gonzaga, Elisabetta's brother, the marquis of Mantua, one of the ugliest young men in Italy. Like the Montefeltros, the Gonzagas made their living as condottieri, Francesco as captain general of the Venetian armies. Although Franceso had been an indifferent, fidgety student, more inclined to riding and hunting than to reading books, and not as bright as Isabella, he, too, had been given a classical education, and had grown up in a palace surrounded by the paintings of Mantegna and such household visitors as Leon Battista Alberti and the poet Angelo Poliziano. At the time Isabella arrived in Mantua, the principality had a very youthful court. Isabella was sixteen, her husband was twenty-five, his two brothers were twenty-one and sixteen, and his sister Elisabetta, who returned often from Urbino for visits, was eighteen.

Soon after Isabella established herself in Mantua, her sister Beatrice was married to Lodovico Sforza, duke of Milan, and thus by ties of blood and alliance Isabella was connected to most of the important powers of northern Italy; she was connected, too, through churchmen among her relatives, to the politics of Rome, and through her friendships among the beautiful people, to Florence, Naples, and many other of the courts of Italy. She cultivated all these connections assiduously by way of correspondence, and, when her husband was off on military business, she administered the affairs of Mantua with a sure touch—as time went on, so sure a touch that it troubled her husband.

Although Isabella and Francesco had not been married for reasons of romantic love, they appear to have grown quite fond of one another early in their marriage. Isabella wrote warm letters to her husband when he was absent, and Francesco, sweetly and amusingly, hired poets to write sonnets for him to give to her as his own. Francesco also had two illegitimate daughters by a mistress; if Isabella had any lovers, she was more discreet about it than her husband.

Isabella suffered her fair share of setbacks, but was rarely unsettled by them. In 1497, her

Often (above), women of Florence busied themselves at odd hours with domestic arts like needlework, spinning, and weaving. Florentine dresses were notable for their elegance.

SCALA

sister Beatrice died in childbirth, having suffered a more severe humiliation than Isabella since Lodovico kept his own stunningly beautiful mistress much in public view at the Milanese court. Isabella continued her correspondence with Lodovico, and when Francesco ran into difficulties with Venice, Isabella arranged to have Lodovico hire her husband. Francesco balked at Lodovico's offer—it did not include the title of captain general of the Milanese army—but Isabella firmly persuaded her husband that the money, about 30,000 florins a year, was more important than the title.

In 1500, having already, to her intense chagrin, borne daughters, Isabella gave birth to a son, thus satisfying her primary duty. The godfather named for the child was Cesare Borgia, a man who richly deserved the evil reputation his contemporaries and history bestowed upon him.

The Borgias were approaching the zenith of their power at this time, and Isabella's brother Alfonso d'Este eagerly married Cesare's sister Lucrezia Borgia. The pope had used his daughter often in pursuit of political alliances: her marriage to Giovanni Sforza was annulled; her marriage to the nephew of the king of Naples ended when the young man was strangled to death in his bed by Cesare's henchmen, with Lucrezia looking on. The Estes at first thought Lucrezia an unsuitable match, but their reservations were dispelled by the offer of a dowry of 300,000 ducats and the reduction of the tribute Ferrara paid as a fief of the Church to a nominal 60 ducats a year.

In 1502, Isabella and Cesare Borgia exchanged friendly but wary letters. Cesare proposed to have his daughter betrothed to Isabella's two-year-old son. On June 12 of that year, Cesare sent off an especially affectionate note to Isabella; on June 13, he set off from Rome with an army to seize Urbino. Duke Guidobaldo and Duchess Elisabetta took refuge with their relatives in Mantua. Isabella was delighted to have Elisabetta stay at Mantua, and welcomed her old friend warmly—and, never neglecting her own interests, wrote Cesare to ask whether she might have, from among the spoils of Urbino, a statue of Cupid by the young Florentine sculptor Michelangelo and a wonderful torso of Venus. She did not, lest it might be so assumed, intend to give these spoils to Elisabetta; she had her own collection that she was eager to augment.

Where should Isabella's loyalties have been placed—with her brother-in-law, and potentially her son's father-in-law, Cesare Borgia, or with her husband's sister and her good friend from Urbino? In fact, Isabella gave her first loyalty to herself. In a world so filled with conflicting loyalties, duties, opportunities, and desires, between one alliance and another, one relative and another, between religion and the demands of the world, between one love and another, sanity all but required an utter consecration to individual interests.

On August 9, 1509, Francesco Gonzaga, having allied himself against Venice with the new Pope Julius II, was leading a company of horse to join a siege of Padua. He had spent the night in a farmhouse, which at daybreak was surrounded by the Venetians. Awakened by a cry of alarm, he dashed out the back door and hid in a field of maize, where he was discovered by four peasants and turned over to the Venetians. He was clapped

into a comfortable jail in Venice, and Isabella ruled Mantua. In an effort to gain Francesco's release from captivity, she appealed for help to King Louis XII of France, to the Emperor Maximilian, and to others, and she endeared herself to the pope by urging an early marriage between one of her daughters and Francesco della Rovere, who was the nephew of both the pope and Guidobaldo. She also refused to be bullied by the Venetians. She instructed the commanders of the fortresses guarding Mantua that they were not to open their gates to the Venetians even if the enemy were to march before them bearing Francesco and murder him in front of their eyes.

She ruled Mantua well in Francesco's absence, and, on his return to his city in 1510, he said, "We are ashamed that it is our fate to have as wife a woman who is always ruled by her head."

Isabella and Francesco were never again warm toward one another. The marquis tried to keep his wife at arm's length, but his own failing health foiled him. Isabella came increasingly to manage the affairs of state, and when Francesco died nine years later, Isabella ruled Mantua through her son. Her notion of rule, according to one of her biographers, Maria Bellonci, was that "the prince must deserve to have the people make his cause their own by making their cause his."

The letters that Isabella wrote in all these years reveal a woman of intelligence, determination, and an insatiable curiosity. She was interested to hear political news, court gossip, word of the latest fashions in jewelry and clothes, wanted to know when she would be able to read the latest installments of Aristo's *Orlando Furioso*, and was one of the exceedingly few people who was interested to hear about Columbus' discovery of the New World. She was impatient to receive anything she asked for, whether information, a pair of silver bracelets, or a new book. "Since I am of an essentially greedy and impatient nature," she chided one poet friend who had promised her a sonnet, "I hold those things the most dear, which I can obtain the soonest." She was often deeply in debt to Venetian bankers for her books and paintings and jewels, and often pawned her jewels to help in one of her husband's wars.

In July of 1501, she wrote to one of her agents

in Venice: "Some Virgils printed in a small size, with minute and almost italic type, have lately been brought here for sale, and please me very much. I hear that the works of Petrarch and Ovid are also to be published, and should like to have them both in parchment."

The Venetian printer who published these books was Aldus Manutius, who was just beginning to print the first of his famous editions of classical authors. Isabella bought the whole series of books that did so much to spread the revival of the classics throughout Europe. When she learned that Aldus was short of parchment, "clear and very white and fine and even, not thick in one place and thin in another," she immediately dispatched a servant to Parma to get the paper for the Aldine Press. She pressed Aldus for more and more of his books, and demanded that he hurry up; but she did not hesitate to haggle with him over his prices.

She was particularly fond of Virgil, Horace, Livy, Pliny, Seneca, Plautus, and Terence. And her intellectual curiosity was not merely a fashionably idle interest. To make sure that the Latin translation of the Psalms was accurate, she commissioned her own translation from the Hebrew. She kept up, too, with the popular literature of her day—the stories of Boccaccio, French romances, the story of the Holy Grail, of King Arthur and the Knights of the Round Table, of Lancelot and Tristan.

Of all the literati who gathered at Mantua, Isabella's favorite was Niccolò da Correggio, twenty-five years her senior, a handsome poet and playwright, an accomplished horseman who often took the honors in tourneys. Isabella's library contained several of his books, including one volume bound in white damask and embellished with diamonds. His literary accomplishments do not seem too impressive today, but Isabella pronounced him the best courtier and the finest poet in Italy. In his turn, Niccolò addressed her as *Madonna unica mia* and when he referred to her in speaking to others called her *la mia illustrissima Isabella*. At last, in a courtly conversation in Milan, like the one Castiglione recorded in Urbino, Niccolò declared Isabella to be *la prima donna del mondo*. It would be nice to think that they were lovers.

Evidently discontented with the world that

Wives retained property rights in law. Above: a judge asks a litigant for proof of her right to a sum of money. Below: two Venetian courtesans, with typically bleached and frizzy hair

had been made for her, Isabella made her own private world out of a suite of rooms on the ground floor of the palace. The studio of the Grottas, as it was called, became the archetypal literary salon. It was decorated with carved and gilded woodwork and majolica pavement, and opened onto a court, decorated in the style called *grottesca*, with stuccoed niches and statues. It was in her studio that Isabella received her sister-in-law Elisabetta of Urbino and her humanist friends, and listened to music and poetry recitals. It was for these rooms that she sought

MUSÉE CONDÉ, CHANTILLY

paintings from Mantegna, Gentile Bellini, Perugino, Lorenzo Costa, Michelangelo, Romano, and Raphael. It may have been here that Leonardo da Vinci, who stopped briefly at Mantua, made his portrait sketch of Isabella.

For the studio, Mantegna painted *Parnassus,* or *The Triumph of Love,* in which Mars and a nude Venus, gently holding hands, preside over dancing women led by Isabella herself. She thought Perugino might paint an allegorical fantasy for her, too, and she knew exactly what she wanted. "Our poetic invention," she wrote to Perugino, "which we greatly want to see painted by you, is a battle of Chastity against Lasciviousness, that is to say, Pallas and Diana fighting vigorously against Venus and Cupid. And Pallas should seem almost to have vanquished Cupid, having broken his golden arrow and cast his silver bow underfoot; with one hand she is holding him by the bandage which the blind boy has before his eyes, and with the other she is lifting her lance and about to kill him. By comparison, Diana must seem to be having a closer fight with Venus for victory. Venus has been struck by Diana's arrow only on the surface of the body. . . ."

Isabella goes on in this fashion for a while and then writes, "I am sending you all these details in a small drawing, so that with both the written description and the drawing you will be able to consider my wishes in the matter."

Perugino, a famous painter, replied meekly that he would do his best.

On occasion, Isabella's wish to have things her way lacks charm. To one artist whom she had commissioned to decorate a small room in the palace, she wrote: "Since we have learned by experience that you are as slow in finishing your work as you are in everything else, we send this to remind you that for once you must change your nature, and that if our *studiolo* is not finished on our return, we intend to put you into the dungeon of the Castello. And this, we assure you, is no jest on our part."

With Leonardo da Vinci, she was more respectful, and less successful. She begged to have a painting from him, "any work," she said to one of her intermediaries. "We would leave the subject and the time to him." Alas, she was informed, "Leonardo's manner of life is very changeable and uncertain, so that he seems to live for the day only. . . . He is working hard at geometry, and is quite tired of painting." Isabella persisted, and was told that "his mathematical experiments have absorbed his thoughts so entirely that he cannot bear the sight of a paintbrush." Still she persisted, and was told that Leonardo "replied that all he could say for the moment was that I might send you word that he had begun to do what Your Majesty desired. This is all that I have been able to obtain from the said Leonardo." Perhaps Leonardo did not care to paint an allegory? Perhaps he would prefer a religious subject? Isabella wrote suggesting a portrait of the twelve-year-old Christ, saying to Leonardo, "If you consent to gratify this our great desire, remember that apart from the payment, which you shall fix yourself, we shall remain so deeply obliged to you that our sole desire will be to do what you wish, and from this time forth we are ready to do your service and pleasure. . . ."

Isabella received another promise or two from Leonardo, but she never received a painting. Nonetheless, she was not often disappointed by her artists and poets and printers and scholars, and she did, at last, manage to make a world very much after her own design. Her life—like the lives, no doubt, of many women of her time—was spent somewhere between the ideal of Castiglione and the harsh lot of the ordinary woman, a life often marked by conflict, by the clash of her desires and of the expectations imposed upon her by her male-dominated world. She exemplified, Maria Bellonci wrote, "the necessity of living according to an inner order that vibrates in continual response to the external world, and by which we surmount the error of facts, the harshness of circumstance, and the inertia of our surroundings." That, too, the ability of men and women to exceed the presumed limitations of their time, is a general characteristic of the Renaissance.

"It seemed impossible," said Lorenzo de' Medici, "that she was loved by so many men without any jealousy and praised by so many women without envy." The lady was Simonetta Vespucci, shown opposite in a posthumous portrait in which the snake around her neck symbolizes her untimely death, at twenty-three, of consumption.

CHAPTER VII

THE SCHOLAR

Isabella d'Este was favored with one of the best educations the Renaissance could provide. Instructed by private tutors drawn from among the finest scholars of the age, her mind was furnished with a knowledge of art and music and letters and, above all, of history and philosophy, so as to make it as different from those of most of her contemporaries and her ancestors as the swirling nudes of Botticelli are from the wooden saints of a previous century.

The fashioning of the modern mind commenced in the fourteenth century with Petrarch, who is known to us today as a great Italian poet, but who was known in his lifetime as a Latin scholar. Born in 1304 in Arezzo, Petrarch was sent to study law at Bologna, where, since the eleventh century, the tenets of Roman law had been used as a model for students. Other bits and scraps of the classical world were kept alive at medieval universities too. Cicero's writings were still used to drum the rudiments of Latin into young students. Aristotle was taught in Latin translation, since his system of logic was deemed useful in theological disputation; Virgil,

Glancing up from his classical texts, the cardinal opposite, a model humanist scholar, sits surrounded by objects which, like those in the trompe-l'oeil wood inlay (inset above), collectively symbolize art, letters, and science.

Ovid, and Horace survived and provided models of rhetoric for future clergymen and lawyers. Petrarch, however, was evidently less struck by the use he could make of Cicero in a legal career than he was by the simple fact that Cicero's fame had survived for centuries. Petrarch abandoned the law and set out to gain fame for himself by writing—in Latin and in the Tuscan vernacular—in the style of the classical authors. In his pursuit of classical texts to serve as models for this new endeavor, he assembled a considerable library, including two items that he treated like religious icons, the works of Plato and Homer in Greek, which he could not read.

When Petrarch stumbled upon a Greek scholar named Leontius Pilatus, the poet turned Pilatus over to his friend Boccaccio, who was interested in classical mythology. Boccaccio took Pilatus to Florence, where the Greek scholar translated Homer, and taught Greek to other young scholars. In fact, his knowledge of classical Greek was very shaky, and the translation he inspired Boccaccio to do of Homer was often nonsensical.

By the beginning of the fifteenth century, the Petrarchan interest in classical authors had been carried throughout Italy. Vittorino da Feltre established a school at Mantua (where he taught Federigo da Urbino), and Guarino da Verona taught Latin and Greek at Ferrara. In

77

Together with painters, sculptors, architects, and composers, poets were accorded much honor in Renaissance Italy. Above, a maiden lifts a laurel wreath preparatory to crowning a poet.

Florence, Coluccio Salutati took up Greek studies and insisted on the relevance of the classical world to his own times. In the history of Republican Rome, Salutati declared, one might study the lives of great men to see how they accomplished their ends—and imitate them. Among Salutati's young disciples were Poggio Bracciolini and Leonardo Bruni, who took their love of the classical (pagan) world to Rome, where they worked in the papal chancery.

This new band of scholars was a scruffy lot. Some were well-born, like Pico della Mirandola, who could afford to travel from university to university and city to city in search of manuscripts and mentors. Most were the bright offspring of poor parents who made their way up in the world with their brains, defended their ideas as tenaciously as a weaver guarded his loom, and batted about in search of jobs and books. Books were essential, of course, and

scarce. Even a well-to-do merchant would rarely have more than a couple of dozen volumes; despite the advent of printed books, many sources remained in manuscript, untranslated from the Greek, or in various manuscripts that required copying and critical comparison. The big libraries belonged to monasteries, to the Vatican, to a rich prince or merchant, to a university—and the scholars clustered around these vital centers of source material.

The more fortunate scholars garnered jobs as tutors in wealthy families, where they were provided with a comfortable room, good food, and access to the all-important library. Others went from university to university, fitting their scholarly pursuits around the demands of teaching. They rose at four or five o'clock in the morning, attended communal prayers, lectured for four hours, had lunch at ten o'clock, taught for another four hours, squeezed in a little work of their own, had supper at five o'clock, and sometimes lectured again before they were able to turn to their own work.

Universities, of which there were about eighty in Europe, were most often haphazard affairs. The famous university of Padua, like many others, had no building of its own and held classes in whatever (cold, uncomfortable) rooms it could find. In browsing through the letters of Renaissance scholars, it often seems that the references to Virgil and Plato are outnumbered by references to indigestion, eye strain, backaches, cold feet, and the lack of good books to be found in the library.

If a scholar became sufficiently popular or famous, he could move on to a more comfortable spot, or, indeed, he could start his own university. He had only to find himself some rooms, a few other popular instructors (who would all bring their students with them), and a new school was founded. Usually, however, after the introduction of printing, fame and comfort depended upon a published book. "Publish or perish" was a dictum of particular force in the Renaissance. A book could be dedicated to a potential patron, and thus secure the author a good place, for instance, in the Medici household, with its promise not only of good books and good food, but also the company of other leading scholars, a glimpse of antique statues, and a sense of being appreciated by the rich and powerful.

The revival of the ancient world was motivated by curiosity, by a fascination with worldly fame, by nostalgia for a golden age in a difficult time, by a hunger for inspiration, and by an appreciation of beauty. Bookworms and aesthetes initiated the revival for which the Renaissance was named, and they secured their revolution by proving to their princely patrons the utility of their intellectual pleasures.

In the 1430's, Pope Eugenius IV was engaged in wrangles and wars with Milan and Naples and other principalities, and was endeavoring to impose his political will on his rivals by appealing to the Church tradition that all worldly leaders owe ultimate homage to the pope. Eugenius' argument rested ultimately on a document, the Donation of Constantine, in which the Emperor Constantine, in the fourth century, allegedly declared that "all the provinces, places, and cities of Italy and the Western regions" should be governed by Pope Sylvester "and his successors."

Lorenzo Valla, a scholar in the service of King Alfonso of Naples, applied the new scholarly discoveries in history, law, and philosophy to the Donation of Constantine and found it to be a forgery. Its vocabulary and semantics dated from a later age; certain towns mentioned in the text were not founded until later; and it contained legal contradictions. The new learning was not only interesting, it was useful, and it became an essential element in the education of any Renaissance ruler, just as arithmetic was essential to a banker.

History was no longer perceived as a working-out of the divine will. It provided legal precedents, examples to be emulated, excuses for actions. Historians saw relationships between causes and effects and, like Machiavelli, used historical events to instruct rulers of their own time. Businessmen embraced the notion that money need not be the tainted product of usury, but the means for shaping a new community of noble proportions. History was used and abused as propaganda. Salutati, living in Florence, liked to recall the days of Republican Rome; in Milan the duke favored scholars who celebrated the great figures of Imperial Rome; in the late fifteenth century in Florence, when the Medicis had completely smothered the republican government, Republican Rome was not often mentioned by writers.

Scholars, merchant-bankers, and rulers vied not only with one another for pre-eminence, but they also vied with the ancients. Who was the best, most famous writer or ruler of the ancient world, and why, what had he done, for what was

In this view of a Renaissance school, the masters eat at the high table, and their students at the low. At such institutions, young Italians of the fifteenth century were led into an entirely new world—that of humanism.

he admired? Which is to be more valued, the active or the contemplative life? Which is the superior art, painting or sculpture? When Guarino da Verona (supported by a duke) attacked the ancient Republican hero Scipio, Poggio Bracciolini (a citizen of the republic of Florence) defended Scipio and attacked Guarino viciously. The questions that scholars debated—often vituperatively—and the knowledge they had were of critical importance. A dynasty might fall, a merchant-prince might not gain immortal fame, if Scipio were preferred to Caesar, or if one failed to patronize architects, or if one favored painters over sculptors, or if one did not write poetry as well as rule a state. It was not merely idle interest that caused the duke of Urbino to surround himself with writers and scholars. Books were collected because they were important; discoveries of manuscripts were hailed as great events.

When Poggio Bracciolini found six orations of Cicero and the first complete Quintilian in an abbey in Switzerland, in "a sort of dungeon, foul and dark, at the bottom of a tower," he copied them all out in thirty-two days. The patrons of these scholars were in a hurry. They were eager, first, for useful things—books about politics, architecture, medicine, geography, natural science. Aristotle's *Poetics*, which had been known as early as the thirteenth century, was not translated until the end of the fifteenth century. The library at Urbino had catalogues of the libraries of Milan, the Vatican, the books Cosimo de' Medici gave to a monastery, and of Oxford, and, in addition to classical texts, contained every work on medicine then known. But the patrons were eager, too, for plays that showed great men engaged in great actions, and Cosimo was so eager to read the works of Plato that he undertook the entire support of Marsilio Ficino so that the scholar could translate the Greek philosopher into Latin. It was around Ficino that the Platonic Academy grew up and discussed the ideal ruler, who—Ficino, Cosimo, and Plato agreed—was a philosopher-king, not an elected republican leader. Far from being a pleasant intellectual diversion, the study of Plato had immediate application to the daily lives of Cosimo and his fellow Florentines.

Because the scholars seemed to possess such

Popes were among the most active supporters of the new learning. Above, Sixtus IV visits the Vatican library, which he enlarged. Note that the books are still laid flat in the medieval manner, rather than placed upright on shelves.

crucial knowledge, they were often allowed a license that others were not, they were often pampered, and they were often reviled. They formed a distinctly new element in society, composed of the well-born and of lowly born scroungers, wanderers in search of manuscripts, masters, jobs, patrons, causes, conversations; they searched among the Roman ruins for clues

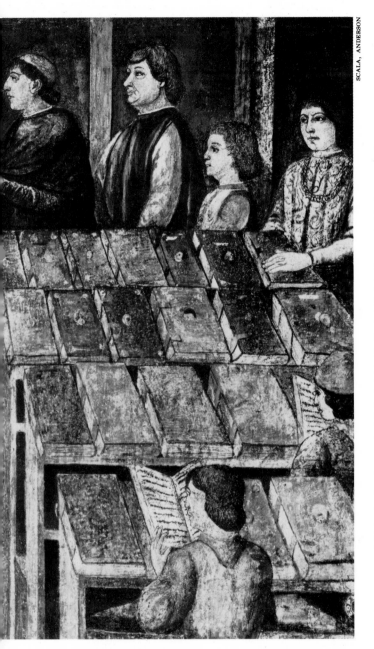

course of his career. When he was reprimanded for his morals by a cardinal, Poggio is supposed to have said, "I have sons, which is very respectable in a layman; and I live without a wife according to the general custom of the clergy."

Francesco Filelfo was, according to his enemy Poggio, the son of a monk and a tripe-seller. An arrogant and disagreeable man, he was once set upon by a bandit who tried to murder him. He believed the Medicis were behind the attempt on his life and advocated the death penalty for Cosimo when the latter was imprisoned by political opponents in 1433. When Cosimo recovered control of the Florentine government, he exiled Filelfo, who fled to Siena, pursued by the would-be assassin (who was caught and had his right hand cut off). This time Filelfo vilified the Medicis, in *The Book of Exile*, as innkeepers, usurers, and promoters of vice, and he then tried to have some of his enemies in Florence poisoned by a hired tough. In the end he made his peace with the Medicis—money could always buy his loyalty—and died after having been appointed a professor at the Florentine university.

Lorenzo Valla, who, after exposing the Donation of Constantine as a fraud, proceeded to discredit other key historical documents of the Church, was finally hired as an official of the papal curia, and upon his death was buried with honors in St. John Lateran in Rome.

Before this loose-knit band of scholars and fellow travelers emerged in Italy, the education of children had been a bleak affair. Even during the Renaissance, perhaps less than one per cent of the working poor were able to read. Those fortunate enough to be able to join a guild learned to read and write as part of their apprenticeship. The elite were schooled in the trivium (grammar, rhetoric, and dialectic) and the quadrivium (arithmetic, geometry, music, and astronomy). The system of education was strictly functional; it trained workers in basic skills and turned out a privileged few for careers in merchant-banking, medicine, law, and the Church. The new learning of the Renaissance was meant to be strictly functional, too: history, geography, philology, philosophy, were found to be necessary for rulers and for merchants dealing with other countries. As time went on, however, the

to the past; they were the first archaeologists; and they advised princes and popes.

Rewards for their work could be handsome. Collucio Salutati became the chancellor of Florence. Bruni, who began life as a poor boy, ended it wearing a scarlet robe with fur-trimmed sleeves, receiving exemption from Florentine taxes, and enjoying the adulation of a claque that followed behind him as he made his deliberate, majestic perambulation through the streets and squares of Florence. Poggio Bracciolini, another poor boy, acquired honors, money, and fourteen illegitimate children in the

His students listen intently as Antonio da Budrio, a noted jurist of Bologna, delivers a lecture. From such schools came two key words for the revival of the classic tradition: **rinascimento** *(renaissance) and* **umanesimo** *(humanism).*

rediscovered ideals of classical education—to shape a whole, well-rounded individual capable of nobility and worldly fame—developed into an end in themselves. The sheer acquisition of knowledge seemed an estimable goal. It seemed, too, that if the ancients could achieve the greatness they did, then so could men and women of the Renaissance. People could improve themselves, shape themselves, form their own nature, and assert their supremacy over the world. No longer the passive victims of divine will, people of the Renaissance believed that they could control their own destiny. The word *humanista* originally meant a teacher of Latin and Greek; by the middle of the fifteenth century, "humanist" had come to mean an individual who believed in the beauty and goodness of a human-centered world.

To bring such a new world into existence required a wholly new approach to education, and new schools and new texts were developed with startling speed. The medieval texts on Latin grammar were replaced by books on science and history, so that students would learn about ancient civilization as they absorbed the language. Valla wrote a new book on linguistic usage, *De Elegantia Latinae Linguae;* other humanists turned out texts on grammar and spelling.

At Mantua, Vittorino da Feltre established a model school, which was variously referred to as the Casa Giocosa (the House of Fun) or the Casa Gioiosa (the House of Joy). The school was supported not by the Church but by the marquis of Mantua, and it was dedicated not to turning out good Christians but to nurturing good humanists. Vittorino continued to teach the old trivium and quadrivium, but he used Virgil and Homer and Plato for texts, and added gymnastics and other physical exercises in accord with the classical ideal of *mens sana in corpore sano.* The well-born from all over Italy were sent to his school, and he himself took in poor students. He varied his curriculum according to the talents of the individual student, saying that "not everyone is good at everything . . . but to each, nature, man's guide and companion, has assigned his task, giving to no one everything, to a few many things, and to everyone something."

After studies with a private tutor or at a school such as Vittorino's, the pupils moved on to a university, where the relative cachet of the disciplines can be measured by the salaries of the professors. In Florence in 1451, the instructor of civil law received 440 florins; the instructor of rhetoric and poetry, useful for diplomats, 350 florins; of medicine 300 florins; of philosophy and morals a mere 70 florins; and of logic 20 florins.

After a stint at the university, a student entered his chosen career, and his advanced education commenced. If he aspired to be accounted a humanist himself, he continued to converse with scholars, to study, to frequent one of the new literary salons, and to read books. The scholars themselves were possessed of a missionary zeal; they believed in education and in the urgent need to popularize and disseminate the fruits of their scholarship. They needed allies, patrons, and printing presses. The goal was to make "everyone lettered and learned" in order to make a new world. Although the scholars constantly, and usually sincerely, insisted that they wished to reconcile pagan and Christian teachings, the Church was not slow to recognize the threat that free thought and expression held for the established order based on the ultimate rule of authority. In 1487, Pope Innocent VIII inaugurated a system of licensing Roman printers. By 1491, religious books were being censored in Venice.

By the time of Leo X, whose pontificate spanned the publication of Luther's ninety-five theses in 1517, full-scale censorship was underway.

Movable-type printing, invented by Gutenberg in Germany, developed quickly in Italy. The first Italian press was established in 1465 in Subiaco. By 1500, there were one hundred and fifty presses in Italy, more than in any other country. Although the presses churned out a great many popular romances, by 1500 there were probably two hundred thousand copies of Virgil in circulation.

The presses became centers of learning as well as of the diffusion of knowledge. Aldus Manutius, from whose press in Venice so many classics issued, provided scholars with bed and board in his own house and had as many as thirty humanists in residence at any given time. At Aldus' dinner table scholars exchanged ideas, suggested projects, commented on one another's work—all in Greek; if anyone slipped into conversation in another language, he was fined. When Erasmus arrived from Holland at Aldus' household in 1508, he ate dinner with Brother Urbano, the

author of a Greek grammar; Marcus Musurus, a professor of Greek literature; Pietro Bembo; and Giovanni Lascaris, who had once collected manuscripts in Greece for Lorenzo de' Medici. Erasmus hated the food, and found he drank too much wine in all this convivial company, but he loved to do his writing in the very midst of the printing shop.

The arguments among all these humanists vying for patrons and publishers and the acceptance of their ideas are famous. One of the more rambunctious fights was a three-way affair among Valla, Bracciolini, and Filelfo. "As Hercules traversed the world," Bracciolini said in one attack on Filelfo, "to benefit mankind by his labors, so you have visited every country and climate to disgust them by your vices." Valla implied in the course of his argument that he had seen military action under Alfonso of Naples.

The scholar's life was not without its hazards. The scene below commemorates an accident that befell a well-known Vatican humanist in Rome, between the Arch of Titus (left) and the Colosseum (right)—an accident he somehow survived.

Giovanni Pico Della Mirandola

"That timid little hare," said Bracciolini, "never saw a naked sword: he dressed up as a kitchen maid and helped the butlers in the army mess. One day an ass kicked him, whereupon he beat the poor creature to death, then started blubbering, believing himself guilty of parricide."

This same style of argument was employed by the young German scholar-monk Martin Luther, who read Valla and Erasmus and applied their philological techniques to the New Testament. By a process of scholarly nitpicking over the translation of the Greek word *metanoia*, Luther initiated the Reformation. *Metanoia*, said Luther, meant "change one's mind," not, as the authorized Church interpretation had it, "do penance." On that niggling little base Luther built a new theology.

The change of mind that occurred in the Renaissance was vast, and, as time went on, people carried with them from day to day a different way of perceiving the world, themselves, the meaning of their houses and activities, their daily business, their ordinary concerns, and their purpose in life. The change can perhaps best be seen by looking inside two minds, one medieval and one Renaissance. Among the medieval rules of daily life set down by Saint Benedict are these:

Not to embrace pleasures.
To become a stranger to the doings of the world.
To suffer persecution for justice's sake.
Not to be proud.
To attribute what one finds good in oneself to God, not to oneself.

84

While his schoolfellows and a dwarf frolic, Massimiliano Sforza heeds his tutor. His was the finest education the

Marsilio Ficino

To recognize on the other hand, that evil is done by
  us, and we should impute it to ourselves.
To long for eternal life with all spiritual desire.
Not to give in to the desires of the flesh.
To hate one's own will.
Not to love frequent and loud laughter.
To obey the commands of the abbot in all things. . . .
To recognize that God knows all things in all places.
To fear the day of judgment.
To be terrified of hell.
To keep the vision of death daily before one's eyes.

And here is Pico della Mirandola, a disciple
of the Platonist Ficino, who took as his life's
goal the mastery of all human knowledge:

Neither a fixed abode nor a form that is thine alone
[Pico imagined God as having said to man] nor any
function peculiar to thyself have we given thee, Adam,
to the end that according to thy longing and according
to thy judgment thou mayest have and possess what
abode, what form, and what functions thou thyself
shalt desire. The nature of all other beings is limited
and constrained within the bounds of laws prescribed
by Us. Thou, constrained by no limits, in accordance
with thine own free will, in whose hand we have
placed thee, shalt ordain for thyself the limits of thy
nature. We have set thee at the world's center that
thou mayest from thence more easily observe whatever is in the world. We have made thee neither of
heaven nor of earth, neither mortal nor immortal, so
that with freedom of choice and with honor, as the
maker and molder of thyself, thou mayest fashion
thyself in whatever shape thou shalt prefer. . . .

"Oh, highest and most marvelous felicity of
man," Pico concludes in his own voice, "to him
it is granted to have whatever he chooses, to be
whatever he wills."

*Renaissance could provide, yet when asked what he wanted
most, he unhesitatingly answered, "Not to go to school."*

85

CHAPTER VIII

THE ARTIST

At the beginning of the fifteenth century, artists were indistinguishable from craftsmen. Sculptors were members of the Guild of Masons, and painters belonged to a branch of the Guild of Doctors and Apothecaries. They were paid the low wages of artisans; they followed the instructions of their patrons to the letter; and they rarely signed their names to their works. By the end of the fifteenth century, artists were regarded as special beings who were endowed with God-like creativity. They signed their works, they improved upon, or sometimes ignored, their patrons' instructions, and they were paid extravagant sums of money. Whereas Botticelli was paid 35 florins for a painting in the late fifteenth century, by 1514 Titian was commanding 2,000 florins for an altarpiece. Michelangelo and Leonardo da Vinci were paid 3,000 florins for paintings in the Florentine Palazzo della Signoria. Lorenzo Ghiberti became so rich that he bought himself a miniature medieval castle—a manor house equipped with a moat and drawbridge. By 1533, Titian was made a count, and among others taken into the nobility were Mantegna, Crivelli, and Bellini. By the middle of the sixteenth century, artists were

Luca Signorelli painted himself (far left, opposite) and Fra Angelico into a religious picture of souls in torment. The depiction of artists as rich citizens shows how their status had risen. Inset above: drafting instruments
MUSEUM OF THE HISTORY OF SCIENCE, OXFORD

accounted such illustrious figures that they were even the subjects of biographies: *The Lives of the Artists* by Giorgio Vasari was a huge best seller in 1568.

Both early and late in the Renaissance, aspiring artists were trained by apprenticeship. Andrea del Sarto was apprenticed at the age of seven to a goldsmith. Titian started at nine, Mantegna at ten. Michelangelo and Botticelli were late starters; both were thirteen when they were apprenticed. Leonardo was an old man of fourteen or fifteen when he began his training. The father of a talented boy often paid a master to take in and train the youngster, and the boy usually joined a large family of the master's own children and other apprentices. They all lived and ate together, and, of course, shared their technical tricks and other innovative ideas. The apprenticeship system ensured that the artists in any given town were an especially closely knit group, communicating discoveries to one another very quickly. In Florence, Lorenzo Ghiberti, a goldsmith whose most famous work is the pair of bronze doors for the baptistery of the cathedral, trained Donatello (who made the first freestanding sculpture since antiquity with his Saint George), Michelozzo di Bartolommeo (architect of the Medici palace), and Uccello (who painted the spectacular *Rout of San Romano* and concentrated on the art of perspective), as well as a number of others.

87

In the 1430's, Cennino Cennini described a model program for an apprentice:

To begin as a shop-boy studying for one year, to get practice in drawing on the little panel; next to serve in the shop under some master, to learn how to work at all the branches which pertain to our profession; and to stay and begin the working up of colors; and to learn to boil the sizes, and grind the gessos; and to get experience in gessoing anconas [the brackets that hold cornices in architecture], and modelling and scraping them; gilding and stamping; for the space of a good six years. Then to get experience in painting, embellishing with mordants, making cloths of gold, getting practice in working on the wall, for six more years drawing all the time, never leaving off, either on holidays or on work days.

In practicing their drawing, the apprentices would spend a good deal of time copying drawings that belonged to the workshop so that the young artists would learn to work in the "house style." The master's set of drawings was a valuable piece of property, sometimes mentioned in wills. In some cases, especially in the instance of drawings related to fortifications or machines or other mechanical devices that artists were called upon to produce, explanatory notes on the drawings were written in code.

This training, which took (in the ideal program at least) thirteen years, prepared an artist to work on walls, canvas, parchment, glass, shell, silk, and wood. In the course of the training, the painter would come to know something—from his master and his fellow apprentices—of architecture, sculpture, and a range of decorative arts. Eventually, Botticelli would paint not only canvases but also wedding chests and banners for processions; others would paint on furniture, manuscripts, horse trappings, and shields. Michelangelo would be a painter, sculptor, architect, and poet.

When Leonardo came to apply for a position in the court of Lodovico Sforza in Milan, he wrote the duke that he could design bridges, cannon, assault machines, mortars, catapults, and "give you as complete satisfaction as anyone else in architecture, in the construction of buildings both public and private, and in conducting water from one place to another. Also I can execute sculpture in marble, bronze, or clay, and also painting. . . ." With his letter, Leonardo presented the duke a silver lyre in the shape of a horse's skull that he had made.

Once an apprentice had learned to work in his

In the early Renaissance the line between arts and crafts was vague. The sculptor immediately to the left, modeling a figure of a child, was, for example, on a level with the masons whose studio he shared. But in time some artists were recognized as such. One was the sculptor Donatello, whose David (right) was the first freestanding nude statue since antiquity.

own master's style, Cennini advised him to "take pains and pleasure in constantly copying the best works that you can find done by the hand of great masters. . . . Then you will find, if nature has granted you any imagination at all, that you will eventually acquire a style individual to yourself. . . ." Ultimately, said Cennini, "the most perfect steersman that you can have, and the best helm, lie in the triumphal gateway of copying from nature. And this outdoes all other models. . . ."

Cennini also had some personal advice for the young apprentices:

Your life should always be arranged just as if you were studying theology, or philosophy, or other sciences, that is to say, eating and drinking moderately, at least twice a day, electing light and wholesome dishes and thin wines. . . . There is [a temptation] which, if you indulge it, can make your hand so unsteady that it will waver more, and flutter far more, than leaves do in the wind, and this is indulging too much in the company of women.

Most of these young apprentices were poor boys. Sodoma's father could afford to pay the boy's master 7 florins a year for 7 years to cover food and lodging and clothes. Michelangelo,

whose father was a farmer, was fortunate enough to become friends with one of Domenico Ghirlandaio's apprentices; and so, at the age of thirteen, having practiced drawing on his own for some years, Michelangelo was able to arrange to have Ghirlandaio's support during his apprenticeship. Ghirlandaio was to pay the boy 6 florins for his first year, 8 for his second, and 10 for his third year.

Often enough, a young apprentice would display a precociousness in his craft that would immediately put an end to his apprenticeship. When Verrocchio received a commission for a painting of the Baptism of Christ, he had the young Leonardo paint in an angel. Leonardo's angel was so fine that it is said Verrocchio never again had the courage to paint anything himself. Leonardo then, like other talented young apprentices, became an active collaborator with his master, a full-fledged member of a workshop that would turn out a variety of objects on commission. Toward the end of the fifteenth century, when paintings emerged from workshops bearing the master's signature, the signature did not always mean that the master himself had painted the work; it meant, rather, that he approved the work and attested that it was up to the standards of his shop. When the master died, he would often bequeath his unfinished commissions to one of his relatives in the trade. Thus the Della Robbia family went on for several generations turning out terra cottas; the Bellini business passed from Jacopo to Gentile to Giovanni.

Because of such arrangments as these, it is frequently difficult to attribute Renaissance paintings or parts of them to the proper painter; and a sculptor might collaborate on work or finish a statue that another had begun. Because of these arrangments, too, artists often gave one another valuable tips. The architect Brunelleschi was intrigued by a rare classical treatise, Vitruvius' *De Architectura,* in which Vitruvius wrote of a means of "pictorial deception" that made buildings appear "to advance and recede" even though they were painted on a flat surface.

Brunelleschi studied this technique of pictorial deception and drew the piazza in front of the Florentine cathedral according to the ancient rules. He had rediscovered the technique of perspective, and he quickly taught his technique to a young friend, the painter Masaccio.

Born just outside Florence in 1401, Masaccio was, according to Vasari, "very absent minded and erratic, and he devoted all his mind and thoughts to art and paid little attention to himself and still less to others. He refused to give any time to worldly cares and possessions, even to the way he dressed. . . . So instead of calling him by his proper name, which was Tommaso [Guidi], everyone called him Masaccio [sloppy Tom]." Masaccio lived only twenty-seven (some say twenty-eight) years, but in that brief span he painted a number of frescoes in the Brancacci Chapel of the church of Santa Maria del Carmine. He applied the principles of perspective to these frescoes and so transformed Western painting. No longer were frescoes to depict rows of flat, two-dimensional saints, lined up one above the other. Paintings henceforth resembled picture windows opening out onto a three-dimensional world with fully rounded human beings placed commandingly in the center.

According to Vasari, "all those who have endeavored to learn the art of painting have always gone for that purpose to the Brancacci Chapel to grasp the precepts and rules demonstrated

Naturalism, secularism, and classicism—"the three revolutionary elements in Renaissance art"—are all present, in some measure, in the pictures on these pages, which together reveal the unique character of that era in Italy. In **The Expulsion of Adam and Eve** *(opposite), painted around 1427, Masaccio put to use the lessons in perspective he had learned from Brunelleschi; instead of the flat, stylized figures of medieval paintings, his are rounded, expressive, intensely human. Perspective is the key, too, to Bellini's architectural study of about 1445 (right) and to Mantegna's* **The Dead Christ** *(below) of about 1490. And in* **The Last Supper** *(bottom) of 1495–98, Leonardo da Vinci added to perspective his sfumato technique, omitting all lines, with telling effect.*

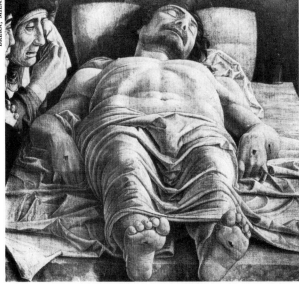

Lorenzo Ghiberti's relief self-portrait (above) appears in a border of one of the bronze doors he created for Florence's baptistery. Michelangelo called his east doors fit to be the portal to Paradise.

by Masaccio. . . ." Vasari specifically mentioned, among many, Fra Filippo Lippi, Filippino Lippi, Andrea del Castagno, Verrocchio, Leonardo da Vinci, Michelangelo, Raphael, Andrea del Sarto.

Each of these artists added another element of realism to painting: greater expressiveness in the faces of subjects, a greater sense of movement and vitality, a more precise, naturalistic rendering of textures, of light and shade, an air of nonchalance, even of humor. Fra Angelico, the supreme colorist, introduced a range of colors that any Florentine cloth merchant could appreciate. Piero della Francesca pointed the way to showing the human body under extreme physical and emotional strain, and he worked out the principles of aerial perspective — creating a sense of distance and depth by making his backgrounds look hazily out of focus. The whole of the physical world was drawn into paintings — manipulated, mastered, and celebrated — and at the center of those paintings were placed bold princes and soldiers and bankers and beautiful women. In the Brancacci Chapel, Masaccio had painted a seminude Christ, with Christ's muscles fully articulated. Donatello, with his statue of

David, made the first nude statue since antiquity. With such precedents, Renaissance artists painted and sculpted nudes in an exhilarating celebration of the beauty — and, as Michelangelo called it, the "nobility" — of the human-centered universe.

Paolo Uccello pursued the study of perspective with a diligence that became a town joke. His wife "told people that Paolo used to stay up all night in his study, trying to work out the vanishing points in his perspective, and that when she called him to come to bed he would say: 'Oh, what a lovely thing this perspective is!'"

The urge to make something that looked absolutely alive seized hold of artists of the Renaissance. It was said of Donatello that while he worked on one statue he kept muttering to it, "Speak, damn you, speak!" And Michelangelo's sculpture of David seems, as one walks slowly toward it from the front, to fill its lungs with air, to breathe.

At last, when Leonardo came to paint the *Last Supper* in Milan, he was able to draw on an accumulation of techniques that made the illusion of reality complete. The figures are rendered in his novel *sfumato* technique, "without lines or borders, in the manner of smoke" — as the human eye naturally sees outlines at a distance. The Apostles, having just heard Christ say, "One of you will betray me," all react vigorously. The painting was done on the wall of a refectory in Milan; and through the windows in the background, one can see the Milanese countryside. The table is positioned as the head table in the room; the architectural detail repeats the architectural details of the refectory itself; and the assumed source of light for the painting was the actual source of light in the room, a row of windows on the wall to the left. When the painting was fresh, monks entering the room for dinner must have been startled. It would have seemed that Christ and the Apostles were very much alive and having dinner at the refectory in Milan.

Such amazing innovations caused a great deal of talk, especially, of course, among artists. The artists were all intensely aware of one another's work, often competitive and often in one another's company. They formed clubs where they drank and ate together, played practical jokes, and told stories about their peers.

The legends passed down to Vasari about Botticelli contain a number of stories of the sort of one-upmanship that Florentines particularly enjoyed. A cloth-weaver once moved into the house next to Botticelli's, and, it was said,

set up no less than eight looms which when they were working not only deafened poor Sandro with the noise of the treadles and the movement of the frames but also shook his whole house. . . . What with one thing and another, he couldn't work or even stay in the house. Several times he begged his neighbor to do something about the nuisance, but the weaver retorted that in his own home he could and would do just what he liked. Finally, Sandro grew very angry, and on top of his roof, which was higher than his neighbor's and not all that substantial, he balanced an enormous stone . . . which threatened to fall at the least movement of the wall and wreck the man's roof, ceilings, floors, and looms. Terrified at the prospect, the cloth-weaver ran to Sandro only to be told, in his own words, that in his own house Sandro could and would do just what he wanted to. So . . . the man was obliged to come to reasonable terms and make himself a good neighbor.

Other artists commenced to display a sense of personal license, an assumption that they themselves were apart from the ordinary run of men. Fra Filippo Lippi, Vasari said, "was so lustful that he would give anything to enjoy a woman. . . . His lust was so violent that when it took hold of him he could never concentrate on his work." Because he often wandered off the job when the urge came upon him, Lippi was once locked in a room by Cosimo de' Medici:

[His] animal desires drove him one night to seize a pair of scissors, make a rope from his bed-sheets and escape through a window to pursue his own pleasures for days on end. When Cosimo discovered that he was gone, he searched for him and eventually got him back to his work. And after that [Cosimo] always allowed him to come and go as he liked, having regretted the way he had shut him up before and realizing how dangerous it was for such a madman to be confined. Cosimo determined for the future to keep a hold on him by affection and kindness and being served all the more readily, he used to say that artists of genius were to be treated with respect, not used as hacks.

When Leonardo da Vinci painted the *Last Supper*, the prior of the Dominican monastery

Lorenzo de' Medici, sculpted above by Andrea del Verrocchio, was the archetype of the patron, whose generosity—and lust for glory—made Renaissance Italy the scene of an unprecedented outpouring of art.

kept pressing the artist to finish, and finally complained to the duke about Leonardo's dilatoriness. The duke sent for Leonardo, and questioned him about the painting, "although [the duke] showed perfectly well that he was only doing so because of the prior's insistence. Leonardo, knowing he was dealing with a prince of acute and discerning intelligence, was willing . . . to explain his mind at length. . . . He explained that men of genius sometimes accomplish most when they work the least; for, he added, they are thinking out inventions and forming in their minds the perfect ideas which they subsequently express and reproduce with their hands. Leonardo was having trouble with painting two heads—one of Christ, since he could not "conceive the beauty and divine grace that properly belonged to the incarnate Deity" and the other Judas, since he could not "imagine the features" of so horrible a man. However, Leonardo said, "he would try to find a model for Judas, and if he did not succeed in doing so, then he was not without the head of that tactless and importunate prior."

The relationship between artists and patrons 93

underwent a vast change in the fifteenth century. Leonardo was courteous to the duke of Milan, but he could afford to ignore letters of Isabella d'Este and not even favor her with a personal refusal of her entreaties for a painting. Nonetheless, as realism is the prime technical characteristic of Renaissance art, so is secularism the prime characteristic of its content, and artists were acutely aware of the demands of the secular world. Nouveaux-riches merchants and bankers still wanted religious scenes for their chapels; but they wanted to have their portraits painted as well, and they also wanted paintings of classical allegories, famous battles, celebrations of weddings and other family occasions. Indeed, Renaissance art was not only secular, it was increasingly casual and colloquial. Patrons and their friends, and friends of the artists, turned up as faces in the crowd at the scene of the Nativity. In the Brancacci Chapel, one could pick out portraits of Donatello, Brunelleschi, the patron Antonio Brancacci, a number of other Florentines, and the convent's porter with a bunch of keys in his hand. Renaissance artists not only revolutionized all sense of time and space, they not only revived the classical world and showed that it was still alive three-dimensionally in a modern Italian landscape, they also showed their contemporaries at home in the ancient world and living on easy, equal terms with it. Indeed, the artists felt so at ease in making up their own worlds that they were able even to paint little inside jokes. When Andrea Mantegna painted a chapel in Padua, his former master, Squarcione, criticized him, saying that the paintings "were inferior work since when he did them Andrea had imitated marble statues. . . . Andrea would have done far better, [Squarcione] suggested, if he had painted his figures not in various colors but just as if they were made of marble, seeing that his pictures resembled ancient statues and such like things rather than living creatures." When Mantegna got around to painting the last scene for the chapel, he "portrayed Squarcione as an ugly pot-bellied figure carrying a lance and sword."

As their pride in their accomplishments increased, artists did not hesitate to "sign" their works by including self-portraits in the whole design. Ghiberti sculpted his own portrait for his bronze doors, and, in one painting of the *Adoration of the Magi,* Botticelli is to be found looking over his shoulder with an arrogant expression on his face, as though affronted by the intrusion of the viewer.

Naturalism, secularism, and classicism were the three revolutionary elements in Renaissance art, and the way in which those diverse influences were combined by the artists reveals the unique character of the Renaissance.

Michelangelo was impressed by the neo-Platonic distinction beween "appearance" and "essence," and, as he developed, he tried increasingly to go beyond mere appearance and reveal the inner essence of his subjects. To paint "a beauty," Raphael said, "I need to see many beauties. . . . But as there is a shortage . . . of beautiful women, I am making use of a certain idea which comes into my mind." "If the painter wishes to see enchanting beauties," Leonardo wrote, "he has the power to produce them. If he wishes to see monstrosities, whether terrifying, or ludicrous and laughable, or pitiful, he has the power and authority to create them. If he wishes to produce towns or deserts, if in the hot season he wants cool and shady places . . . he can make them. If he wants valleys, if from high mountaintops he wants to survey vast stretches of country . . . he has the power to create all this. . . . Indeed, whatever exists in the universe, whether in essence, in act, or in the imagination, the painter has first in his mind and then in his hands. . . ."

Art, as the historian Peter Laven has written, "did not imitate nature in the ordinary sense; it rather imitated the creation of nature." It was, in short, a God-like activity. The humanists were able to tell the artists that Cicero had said painting was not an imitative but a creative art, and Dürer was able to say that art consisted of the ability to "pour out new things which had never before been in the mind of any other man." Inspired by classical sources, then, the Renaissance artists created a material world that surpassed the creation of God Himself. It can be no wonder that Titian was made a count, or that merchant-bankers, who were also the creators of a new material world, showered money on Leonardo for helping to prove how right and beautiful the new material world could be.

In The Architect's Studio, *the painter Bernardino Poccetti documented the re-emergence from obscurity of a profession whose practitioners largely shaped the cities of Renaissance Italy.*

Medieval builders had, as a rule, been anonymous craftsmen, but with the imitation of antique models in construction came a revival of the old Roman term—and concept—"architect."

95

CHAPTER IX

FESTIVITIES

Giovanni de' Medici, the son of Lorenzo and the brother of the Giuliano who spoke on behalf of women in Castiglione's *Courtier,* was elected pope in 1513 and took the name Leo X. Among his many aims as head of the Church, not the least important was to extend Medici political power to territories outside Florence. He determined to create a principality for his brother Giuliano, composed of some combination of Modena, Reggio, Parma, Piacenza, and possibly even Ferrara and Urbino— in which Isabella d'Este had strong family interests. In the autumn of 1514, Isabella decided to pay a visit to Rome.

The marchioness of Mantua was met at Bolsena, sixty miles outside Rome, by Bernardo Bibbiena, another of Castiglione's courtiers, recently made a cardinal by Leo X. Bibbiena presented Isabella's major-domo with 500 ducats —and a promise of more if it was necessary— and escorted her to Rome. There the pope shrewdly asked her to sit beside him and reign as the queen of the season. Before Isabella could engage the pope in serious political talk, she was launched into the social swirl of Rome and dazzled by aristocratic bread and circuses. Like

The giuoco del calcio, *a kind of football played in a public square (opposite), was popular with spectators of all classes. The waiters at a banquet (inset above) symbolize the taste for high living that characterized the aristocracy.*

the Italian rabble who were kept content with such artfully contrived jollities during the trials and upheavals of the Renaissance, Isabella had a wonderful time.

"Yesterday," one of Isabella's ladies-in-waiting wrote home, "the Very Reverend Cardinal Riario gave us a supper so extraordinarily sumptuous that it might suffice for all the queens in the world. We sat for four full hours at the table, laughing and chatting with the most reverend cardinals."

"Sweet and savoury, pastry and game, were all served at once and the same time," one historian has written of such banquets, "whilst the spirit of vulgar ostentation was satisfied by endless courses of rich dishes, so that only the trained gluttons of the time, such as Fra Mariano, were able to do them justice." Fra Mariano, Leo's court jester, was a celebrated wit who entertained at court by sucking four hundred eggs at one time, or eating a camel's-hair coat, or simply running down the middle of the table knocking cardinals on their heads.

Isabella's banquet was modest compared to one given for her mother-in-law some years earlier in Rome. The banquet for Eleanora of Aragon lasted seven hours and ran through "imperial eagles in sugar," gilded oranges (gold and silver gilt were thought to be good for the heart), crab apples, minced chicken livers, capons in white sauce, capons in purple sauce, capons in gelatine, capons in parsley sauce, geese, a

97

live bear, peacocks, lamb, rabbit, pheasant, a whole deer, sturgeon, eels, almond soup, marrow soup, tarts, ices, fruits, marzipan—all topped off with more capons, along with dancers, minstrels, recitations of poetry, and allegorical pantomimes. At a dinner at the palace of the Roman banker Agostino Chigi, the silver plates were thrown out the window after each course so that the guests would know they were given clean silver with each course. In some towns, such feasts as these were held in open-air loggias, and the guests would toss leftovers out into the crowd of hungry peasants who watched the rich gorge themselves.

At a dinner at Cardinal Cornaro's, according to a Venetian envoy:

There was an endless succession of dishes, for we had sixty-five courses, each course consisting of three different dishes, all of which were placed on the board with marvelous speed. Scarcely had we finished one dainty, than a fresh plate was set before us, and yet everything was served on the finest of silver, of which his Eminence has an abundant supply. At the end of the meal we rose from the table gorged with the multiplicity of the viands and deafened by the continual concert, carried on both within and without the hall and proceeding from every instrument that Rome could produce—fifes, harpsichords, and four-stringed lutes in addition to the voices of hired singers.

Music was pervasive during the Renaissance. Street musicians wandered from town to town singing ballads of love and gossip. Guild members had their own songs, as did students and soldiers. Festivals and holy days were always occasions for music, and Lorenzo de' Medici wrote a popular carnival song, with a refrain advising everyone to be happy in the present since the future is always uncertain (*Chi vuol esser lieto, sia/ di doman non c'è certezza*). Towns employed permanent bands of fifers and drummers and trumpeters. Churches, of course, had choirs, and most had organs. Children of well-to-do parents were taught to sing and play an instrument (usually the lute), and after 1500, sheet music was printed and widely distributed. On voyages of trade and discovery, sailors took trumpets and drums with them.

Secular music was the rage, and Europe abounded in composers—from Dufay and Josquin des Prés to Pope Leo X himself. Music was fashionably regarded as the supreme art, and not surprisingly, for it combined two favorite Renaissance ideals: rationalism in its formal basis and emotional immediacy in its content. Composers and performers experimented with new forms, and were amply rewarded. Leo paid one lutenist almost 300 florins a year, and made him a count. He made another musician an archdeacon, and yet another an archbishop. The pope was often to be found sitting in the Sistine Chapel under Michelangelo's ceiling, not praying but with his hands folded in his lap, his eyes closed, listening to a choir he had imported from France or Greece, and humming quietly. Harmony, sweetness, and emotional expressiveness were much praised, and music was thought to be good for everything, from curing illness to causing ecstasy—for the good of man, not, as in "the old music," in praise of God.

While Isabella was in Rome, she was treated to a performance of *Calandria*, which had been adapted by Cardinal Bibbiena from a classical comedy. The plot of Bibbiena's play revolved around identical twins, a boy and a girl, and their love affairs, and the way in which the boy (disguised as a girl) worked his way into the house of his mistress, and the girl (disguised as a boy) was mistaken for a man and, to her amusement, was brought to bed with a woman. In the course of the play women bed down with women, men (mistaking men for women) try to bed down with men, and, at one point, both twins are taken for hermaphrodites. The sexual confusion doubtless appealed to a Vatican court that was in theory celibate but in fact supported an army of prostitutes.

Like music and the other arts, theater was secularized in the Renaissance. Traveling groups of players continued to perform mystery plays on religious holidays, but even religious drama was having its spiritualism and symbolism undercut by the new naturalism. In some Passion plays, the Christ figure had to appear to be covered with welts from the flogging and had to seem to be truly bleeding from the nail wounds. Whether the story of the play was drawn from the Bible or the lives of the saints, a good deal of the dialogue was colloquial, secular, and up to date in its references. Miraculous endings and other-worldly influences were increasingly replaced,

In the form of boxing known as civettino, *one boxer pinned another in place with his foot, and the two slugged it out.*

too, with down-to-earth motivations of jealousy, greed, lust; the old Seven Deadlies, with a new psychological realism.

Most Italians saw their theater in the streets and piazzas. The upper classes were entertained in their own palaces, and, there, both style and content were thoroughly secular. Stage sets were designed according to the new discoveries in perspective, giving rise to the three-walled box set that has characterized naturalistic theater to our own day. Machiavelli was unquestionably the best playwright of the Renaissance. He believed that the purpose of comedy was "to hold up a mirror to domestic life," and his play *Mandragola* can be staged today without changing a word. The plot of *Mandragola* involves a young man, Callimaco, who has fallen in love with the childless, vigorous young wife of a foolish old man. The young man bribes a priest (who is eager to take part in any corrupt scheme) to tell the old man that his wife will conceive a child if she will take a potion made with mandragola, or mandrake root—except that the *first* man to sleep with her after she has taken the potion will die. The priest offers to find a man to perform

the unwelcome duty—and so young Callimaco succeeds. Moreover, after Callimaco makes love with the young woman, he reveals the entire plot to her. She, offended by the behavior of her husband and the priest, thereupon gives Callimaco a key to her house so that he may come as often as he likes.

Angelo Poliziano, Lorenzo de' Medici's poet friend, had the unique misconception that Greek plays had actually combined dialogue and musical elements and that dialogue was meant to be sung. He thought he was reviving Greek theatre with his *Orfeo*, staged about 1480, when he had the actors sing their lines; he had, in fact, produced the first opera.

The Mantuan ambassador wrote to Isabella's husband after they had seen *Calandria:* although "the perfection of mind and purity of life of Madama" were evident for all to see, the ambassador did not think the marchioness should stay any longer in Rome. The city was too full of temptations. Isabella, however, could not bear to leave. Castiglione was escorting her around the Roman ruins, the great inspiration of the humanists, and, as Isabella wrote her husband, "every

day we visit the antiquities, and every day they seem more wonderful."

Isabella was evidently spared a few of the less refined entertainments of the Renaissance. She was not, as far as we know, enticed into any of the gambling games so popular at the time, though she had been in the presence of one of the more avid gamblers of the day in Cardinal Riario. The cardinal had once taken 14,000 ducats from Franceschetto Cibò in two dice games. Loaded dice and marked cards were familiar objects in Rome, as they were elsewhere. It was an easy matter to find someone who would take a bet on, say, the identity of the next pope or the life expectancy of a prince. Genoa and Venice anticipated twentieth-century governments by profiting from the urge to gamble; both set up state lotteries.

Isabella was also spared the exhausting pleasures of the hunt, a popular Renaissance pastime and one of Pope Leo's special passions. Leo was accustomed to setting out from Rome with dozens or hundreds of friends and hangers-on, and spending weeks or months at one of his hunting villas. On these occasions, the staff would provide pens full of jays, herons, and doves to be set loose for those partial to hawking, and beaters would enclose vast areas of wooded valleys for those who fancied the spear and the arrow and the gun. When the hunters were ready, the beaters would drive every large and small frightened creature toward the hunters, and, in a frenzy of yapping dogs, yelling beaters, blowing horns, and the cries of wounded hunters, the outdoorsmen would dispatch boar, wolf, goat, deer, rabbit, and bustard. Cardinals would be gored, violent fights would break out among the beaters, and Leo X would sit atop a hill on his white horse, holding a monocle with white-gloved hand to a nearsighted eye, smiling happily. After the hunt, the valley would be slippery with blood, littered with wounded and dead animals and men, all softly lit by a sweet, dying *mezzogiorno* sun. Leo was never happier than on such days as these.

Outside Florence's baptistery (the octagonal, striped building in the background at left), couples parade, celebrating an important wedding. The banners tied to the trumpets of the musicians (left) display the lily of Florence.

Not all falconers and hunters were as blood-thirsty as Leo X, yet an undeniable strain of violence runs through many Renaissance sports, and the violence is not far below the surface. The modern game of football is a genteel, ritualized pastime compared to the *calcio* of the Renaissance, in which two unruly mobs punched and kicked one another in a sort of riot with a ball. The *palio*, or horse race, was customarily held in a town's central piazza. Jockeys rode bareback over the stone paving of the piazza, following a roughly circular course that, because of an eccentrically placed building or two, frequently had a couple of hazardous hairpin turns. The riders whipped and kicked and screamed at other horses and riders, too. Winning was vitally

important, but, even in the calm re-enactments of the *palio* held for tourists today, the real fun is to see who will be killed in the race, whether horse, or rider, or one of the spectators on those hairpin turns.

Those who missed the *palio* could watch the public tortures and executions. Criminals were sometimes to be seen hanging in cages from municipal towers. While they were in the cages, for as much as two months, they were fed on bread and water; once freed, they had often lost the use of their legs, if nothing else. Capital punishment was often meted out—by hanging or decapitation. Heretics were burned. According to the historian John Gage, in the year before Isabella visited Rome, a priest in Venice was

beheaded, or almost beheaded. After several blows of the ax, the executioner thought he had finished the job and strung the man up on the gallows. A few moments later the man began to move, and so the spectators took up stones and stoned the man to death. It was said that, judging by the expression on the man's face, "he felt his death cruelly."

Marriage celebrations, says Gage, were often "spiced by exhibitions of *The Knight of the Cat*, a spectacle where a man with shaven head and stripped to the waist was shut in a cage with an infuriated cat, which he had to provoke and then kill with his teeth, making no use of his hands. The spectators would incite the combatants with whistles and catcalls, and pelt the cage with melon rind. . . ."

The carnival season came, and Isabella still occupied the place of honor in Leo's court. There was a procession of triumphal cars and a regatta on the Tiber River, and, for comic relief, pigs in barrels were rolled down a steep hill into a crowd of peasants who fought one another savagely for porkers to take home. At Carnival time, in all the cities of Italy, the entire repertoire of Renaissance entertainments was spilled into the streets: minstrels and jugglers competed for audiences with outdoor plays and pageants, sham assaults on wooden castles, fireworks, parades, and the like. One year in Viterbo, for the Feast of Corpus Christi, a model of Christ's tomb was set up in the central piazza, and, after eighteen angelic boys sang, a boy angel came swinging down a rope and, with a sudden dazzling explosion of gunpowder, a sandy-haired young man stepped out of the tomb. For the feast of the Florentine patron saint, Saint John the Baptist, Florence was decked out with banners of silk and cloth of gold and religious pictures; priests bearing sacred relics wound through town in a procession; laymen dressed as angels and saints followed; singers and musicians joined the parade; giants walked about on

---

As a servant enters, ceremoniously holding aloft the next course, some diners at an outdoor banquet (opposite) look up while others show no interest. Such occasions were accompanied by music and dancing—and even by plays, often farces, with the players, like the ones on this page, in elaborate and colorful costumes.

stilts; angels and devils battled in plays and pantomimes.

During the carnival season the trimphal car, or "float," dominated the processions. These processions derived from the ancient custom of triumphal chariot parades. Artists and architects, of the stature even of Brunelleschi and Leonardo, were dragooned into working up cars celebrating the ages of man, or stories from ancient Roman history, pagan gods and goddesses, Eros in swaddling clothes, Bacchus singing obscene songs. On one such occasion, Luca Landucci noted in his diary, "they talked of a cost of 70,000 florins and more for these perishable things that pass like a shadow. . . ."

Such celebrations were good times for thieves —many a partygoer returned to a burglarized house—and for outbreaks of plague. Piero di Cosimo, one of the Florentine painters who was especially adept at designing trimphal cars, once made a grisly Triumph of Death. The figure of Death, surrounded by coffins and torches, stood atop the car. The car itself was painted

MARIO PEROTTI

NATIONAL GALLERY, LONDON

Backgammon—an ancient game from the Near East already well known in classic Greece and Rome—became popular in Renaissance Italy.

with crosses and bones, and, whenever the car stopped in the parade, skeletons got out and chanted dreadful dirges and beat muffled drums.

When Leo X was elected pope, he masterminded his own celebratory parade from the Vatican to the church of St. John Lateran and back. He was preceded by scarlet-clad men-at-arms, members of the cardinals' households, minor prelates, standardbearers of various sorts, one hundred nobles in scarlet silk and ermine, one hundred Roman barons, armed servants, sacristans, pages, Vatican bureaucrats, two hundred and fifty bishops and abbots, the College of Cardinals, two hundred Swiss Guards, and a miscellaneous assortment of Italy's leading citizens. They rode and traipsed through streets decorated with banners and hangings, hastily built triumphal arches mixing Christian martyrs and pagan gods festooned with myrtle (for joy), holly (foresight), and laurel (success). As Leo made his way through the streets, he alternated bestowing his benediction and throwing fistfuls of gold and silver coins to the crowds.

"In thinking over all the pomp and lofty magnificence I had just witnessed," one Florentine wrote home, "I experienced so violent a desire to become Pope myself that I was unable to obtain a wink of sleep or any repose all that night. No longer do I marvel at these prelates desiring so ardently to procure this dignity, and I verily believe every lackey would sooner be made a Pope than a Prince."

Leo's predecessor as Supreme Pontiff had been a big spender in war and patronage of the arts, but he had been a fiscally prudent pope, too. He had left the Vatican treasury with its largest surplus since the Black Death. On this one procession Leo spent fully one-fourth of the treasury's funds. By the end of his eight-year pontificate, the Vatican was 850,000 florins in debt. Centuries before "conspicuous consumption" was identified by an economist, the Renaissance Italians had mastered it. The greatest entertainments of the Renaissance—the ones that diplomats and commoners, diarists, and letter writers all preferred to talk about—were the ones that involved the risk of death and cost a fortune.

On the last night of Isabella's stay in Rome, she was the pope's guest of honor at a festival in the Piazza Navona. There, under eerie torchlight, triumphal cars passed by with the obligatory pagan deities, camels and other exotic animals from the Vatican zoo were trotted through the piazza, and two hundred young men marched as Roman soldiers—muscular, half-naked. Exploding rockets and other fireworks lit the sky, confetti showered down; the crowd was drunk and happy. Isabella left Rome thoroughly entertained.

As for Isabella's diplomatic mission, it failed. She was unable to secure a promise from Leo about the towns she wished to save from his dynastic ambitions, or even to learn what the pope had in mind. As it turned out, Leo changed his mind anyway. In April of 1516, he seized Urbino, sending his old friend the Duchess Elisabetta scurrying to Isabella for a place to stay. The ducal household of Urbino was so strapped they had to melt down their silver plates. Nothing, however, could stop Renaissance festivities. Isabella raised new taxes in Mantua, pawned her jewels, and, in the autumn of that year, she and her friends rejoiced that Castiglione was finally to be married. Isabella and Elisabetta gave a party together, and all the courtiers were there, "and many French gentlemen," and a play called *Gog and Magog*, commissioned for the occasion from a young Mantuan poet, was performed in the presence of "the whole court, and Monsignore de St. Poe, and. . . ."

Tournaments — medieval contests governed by the code of chivalry — continued to be held well into the sixteenth century.

CHAPTER X

THE CHURCH

Religious festivals were fun. To dance in the spring, to sing, to join in parades, to see brightly costumed cardinals and fantastical trimphal cars, were all, first and last, fun. Yet the festivals were also an expression of a pervasive religious feeling that, despite the worldliness of the Renaissance, refused to die. More than four-fifths of the paintings done in the fifteenth century were concerned with religious subjects. Nearly half of the books printed before 1500 were religious books. The mother of Christ and the lives of the saints were memorialized in inexpensive prints and in pamphlets. Every large city had its cathedral; there were 265 episcopal sees in Italy; most large cities had other large churches, monasteries, Church hospitals, and orphanages; every small town had its church. In the mid-fifteenth century, the Church owned perhaps one-third of all Florentine real estate. Streets were decorated with pictures of saints, an occasional crucifix, a miniature shrine.

Religious pictures were to be found in virtually every home; religious symbols decorated doorways, bedsteads, chimneys. Church bells marked the progress of the day, and morning Mass and evening Vespers were well attended.

SCALA

Ignoring his vows, a monk breaks his fast at an inn, where he is served by a comely young woman (opposite). The Church's standards of conduct were lax at all levels, yet the religious feeling evident in the inset above remained a reality.

Birth, marriage, and death were surrounded by religious ritual. A good many Italians were connected to the Church, too, through relatives who had become monks or nuns or priests. The daily life of most Italians was inseparable from the Church.

By the same token, the Church was inseparable from the daily life of most Italians—and so was marked by all the ambition, greed, and worldliness characteristic of the Renaissance family. The Church was so interwoven with the fabric of ordinary life as to be too often indistinguishable from the secular world. Clergymen at all levels, as John Hale has written, could be differentiated "from the lay environment from which they were recruited . . . by little more than a cassock and a theoretical celibacy." Doubtless, many men and women took orders out of deep religious conviction. Many others—the ones their contemporaries most often spoke about—entered the monasteries for regular meals, a hope of improving their social status, a desire to be in the center of Vatican politics. Young women were often put in nunneries to reduce their fathers' dowry burdens, or to thwart unsuitable love matches.

Once in the Church, most monks and nuns learned scarcely more about their religion than their lay relatives. A good monk or priest might be good, but he was no better able to explain a knotty theological problem than any other man. The Church mirrored the hierarchical social

107

structure of the secular world, and the parish priests, drawn from the illiterate lower classes, remained illiterate. Cardinals, drawn from the aristocracy and the nouveaux riches, remained horsemen and huntsmen and givers of banquets. Educated churchmen addressed themselves to each other.

Men and women did not leave the world when they entered the Church. We imagine monks rising early in their Spartan cells, shuffling into chapel for morning prayers, working silently in their gardens during the morning, stopping for more prayer and meditation, dwelling in a different sense of time—and all this is true. Yet it is also true that once their religious duties had been performed (in perhaps no more time than most men and women devoted to their families), clergymen lived in much the same world as laymen. Monks farmed; their superiors kept account books; administrators watched over Church lands, made real-estate deals, bargained with governments, entertained distinguished citizens at feasts. Parish priests were dependent upon fees for weddings and burials, the drawing of wills, votive Masses, and other pastoral services; and many shared the entrepreneurial instincts of their lay brethren. Discipline was lax; concubinage, an open secret. Jokes were rife about monks and priests who were fat, who were drunk from tippling Mass wine, whose cassocks were of particularly fine cloth, whose fingers were covered with rings. Laymen suspected confessors of becoming too intimate with their wives. Nunneries often served as centers of debauchery.

Pietro Aretino, Gentile Sermini, and Tommaso Guardati (known as Masuccio Salernitano) are especially known for their anticlerical stories about monks visiting nuns in their nunneries, selling fake holy relics, staging phony miracles. Of the Minorites, who traveled around Italy begging alms, Masuccio wrote: "They cheat, steal and fornicate, and when they are at the end of their resources, they set up as saints and work miracles, one displaying the cloak of St. Vincent, another the handwriting of St. Bernardino, a third the bridle of Capistrano's donkey." Some "bring with them confederates who pretend to be blind or afflicted with some mortal disease, and often touching the hem of the

Born Rodrigo Borgia, Alexander VI (above) was the father of the infamous Cesare and Lucrezia Borgia. According to the chronicler Vasari, he did not hesitate, as pope, to have his young mistress Giulia Farnese painted as the Madonna.

monk's cowl, or the relics which he carries, are healed before the eyes of the multitude. All then shout 'Misericordia,' the bells are rung, and the miracle is recorded in a solemn protocol." Another useful trick that itinerant preachers employed was to place an accomplice in the audience. In the midst of the priest's sermon, the accomplice would shout "liar," and other abuse at the preacher. The accomplice would then fling himself to the gound as though possessed by the devil—and then the preacher would drive out the devil and be seen to cure his accomplice.

The preaching and begging orders were despised for their petty sins. The Dominicans,

To pay for buildings, art, and private expenditures, popes borrowed from the German banking family of Fugger. The petition above from the Fuggers, asking for religious indulgences, bears Alexander VI's approval at lower right.

who had been organized to stamp out heresy in the thirteenth century, were hated as spiritual police. But aloofness from the day-to-day world was no guarantee of popularity either. The Benedictines, according to one of their own members named Firenzuola, were "well-fed gentlemen . . . [who] do not pass their time in bare-footed journeys and in sermons, but sit in elegant slippers with their hands crossed over their paunches, in charming cells wainscoted with cyprus-wood. And when they are obliged to quit the house, they ride comfortably, as if for their amusement, on mules and sleek horses. They do not overstrain their minds with the study of many books, for fear lest knowledge might put the pride of Lucifer in the place of monkish simplicity."

The Church had a hierarchical structure, of course, but not one that reflected a spiritual hierarchy so much as it mirrored the social hierarchy of the secular world. Well-born girls inhabited proper convents. One convent in Florence had a Medici abbess and nuns from the Cavaleanti, Altoviti, Guasconi, and other leading Florentine families. Bishops were almost invariably drawn from upper-class families, and made wonderful targets for class hatred. Cardinals were spectacularly corrupt, and incorrigible. In 1497, when the bad reputation of churchmen had come to worry even the pope in an absent-minded way, Alexander VI issued a papal bull calling for such reform measures as limiting cardinals to eighty household servants and thirty horses, and forbidding them from being in tournaments. The papal bull was ignored.

109

Much of what we know about the corruption of the Church has been given to us by early Protestants, who were antagonistic to Rome, and by various political enemies of the Borgias or the Della Roveres or the Medicis. Even allowing for the bias of the historical record, however, life at the top in the Renaissance Church was stunning. Church offices were bought and sold, Vatican rivals were assassinated, cardinals led armies in wars of conquest for private ambitions, sumptuous palaces were built. Vice chancellor Rodrigo Borgia's palace was, according to Cardinal Sforza, "splendidly decorated":

The walls of the great entrance halls were heavy with tapestries depicting various historical scenes. A small drawing room led off this, which was also decorated with fine tapestries; the carpets on the floors harmonized with the furnishings which included a sumptuous bed upholstered in red satin with a canopy over it, and a chest on which was laid out a vast and

With the loss of the Church's moral authority an ascetic monk, Girolamo Savonarola, became Florence's ruler; but four years later, tiring of his harsh rule, the Florentines hanged and burned him in the Piazza della Signoria (above).

beautiful collection of gold and silver plates. Beyond this there were two more rooms, one heavy with fine satin, carpeted, and with another canopied bed covered with Alexandrine velvet; the other even more ornate with a couch covered in cloth of gold. . . .

When Giovanni de' Medici first set out for Rome, as a young cardinal, not yet Pope Leo X, his father thought it necessary to write a letter of advice: "I well know that as you are now to reside at Rome, that sink of all iniquity, the difficulty of conducting yourself [well] will be increased. The influence of example is itself prevalent. . . . There is at present little virtue among your brethren of the college. . . ."

110

The higher one advanced in the Church, it seemed, the greater were the opportunities for more flamboyant corruption. In 1513, Erasmus of Rotterdam, having paid a visit to Italy and been shocked by the morality of the southern Europeans, wrote his *Julius Exclusus*, a little fantasy in which Pope Julius is excluded from heaven by Saint Peter. When asked to declare just how he thinks he has deserved entry into heaven, Julius tells Saint Peter (though he is loath to talk to a mere fisherman, and a Jew at that) that he defeated Venice and Bologna, killed many Frenchmen, built many buildings, and left a surplus in the Vatican treasury. Thoroughly impressed with himself, Julius concludes:

You should see the Pope carried in his golden chair by his soldiers with the crowds adoring as he waves his hand. Hear the boom of the cannon, the notes of the bugle, the beating of the drums. See the engines of war, the flames of the torches. Hear the acclaim of the populace, see the loftiest princes kissing the blessed feet of the Pope. Behold the Roman pontiff placing the golden crown on the head of the emperor, the king of kings. . . . What spectacles! Chariots, horses, troops, comely boys, torches flaring, dishes steaming . . . trophies, booty, shouts rending the heavens, trumpets blaring, coins tossed to the crowds, and me as well nigh a god, the author and head of it all. . . .

Italians had dealt with Church corruption for centuries either by simply holding the contradictions in balance and shrugging at the stupendous variety of human nature, or by turning inward to personal mysticism and asceticism. During the Renaissance, however, it appears that Italians increasingly perceived organized religion and genuine religious feeling to be quite separate phenomena; as the institution appeared ever more divorced from religious experience, religion came increasingly to be an individual, rather than an institutional, preserve.

Astrology, demonology, and witchcraft thrived. Even the most sophisticated were divided on the subject of astrology. Among Lorenzo de' Medici's friends, Marsilio Ficino subscribed to the tenets of astrology, while Pico della Mirandola wrote a fierce, rationalistic attack on astrology. Sophisticated men and women were also attentive to portents and omens. Armies went to war on a day deemed appropriate by astrologers by

Right: the Medici arms and the crown of the papacy together grace the cover of a papal bull issued in the year 1520 by Leo X (below), born Giovanni de' Medici. Directed at a certain German critic of the practice of selling indulgences, it was called "Against Martin Luther and His Followers."

marching out of town on a lucky street. Fateful events occurred on Saturdays. If mad dogs were loose, a magical formula had to be repeated on three successive Saturdays. If a hunting falcon did not return home, if a horse sprained its ankle, if a goose caught the pip, all were warning signs of some unknown evil to come. When Lorenzo de' Medici lay dying, lightning struck the Florentine cathedral and knocked some stones loose. Lorenzo wished to know on which side of the cathedral the stones had fallen. When he learned they had fallen in the direction of his palazzo, he took it as an omen. Pictures of the Virgin were seen to weep, or move their eyes. In 1478, Burckhardt has written, "When Piacenza was visited with a violent and prolonged rainfall, it was said that there would be no dry weather till a certain usurer, who had been lately buried in San Francesco, had ceased to rest in consecrated

111

Throughout the Renaissance monks like the ones above farmed the Church's holdings, which included some of the richest lands in all Italy.

earth. As the bishop was not obliging enough to have the corpse dug up, the young fellows of the town took it by force, dragged it round the streets amid frightful confusion, and at last threw it into the Po."

Far from countering such stories, monks and priests spread them. Church dogma and what people believed were often entirely different—and the theologians no longer commanded the respect of the devout.

They made as many partitions and divisions in hell and purgatory [Erasmus said of theologians in *The Praise of Folly*] and described as many different sorts and degrees of punishment as if they were personally acquainted with the situation of these infernal regions. . . . Do not wonder, therefore, that at public disputations they bind their heads with so many caps one over another; for this is to prevent the loss of their brains, which would otherwise break out from their uneasy confinement.

Translations of Virgil did not always ensure rational, classical thoughts; men and women liked to open their volumes of Virgil at random and extrapolate omens from the passages found by chance. Poggio Bracciolini believed in ghosts,

112

and it was well known that the Visconte Palace was haunted.

Witchcraft burgeoned during the Renaissance, and so did the burning of witches. In 1485, forty-one witches were burned at Como. The witches advertised themselves as being particularly adept at sorting out love affairs by including love, hatred, and abortion. According to Burckhardt, the prostitutes of Rome capitalized on the belief in witchcraft by laying in stocks of "hair, skulls, ribs, teeth, dead men's eyes, human skin, the navels of little children, the soles of shoes and pieces of clothing from tombs. They even went themselves to the graveyard and fetched bits of rotten flesh, which they gave their lovers to eat."

The clergy tried from time to time to stamp out these practices, but they were ineffective and were often regarded as mere business rivals. One witch complained that "monks balk me of my gains by explaining dreams, appeasing the anger of the saints for money, promising husbands to the girls, men-children to the pregnant women, offspring to the barren, and besides all this visiting the women at night when their husbands are away fishing, in accordance with the assignations made in day-time at church."

At other times, the Church simply absorbed popular notions and passions. The idea that the Virgin Mary had been immaculately conceived was approved by Pope Sixtus IV. The notion that Mary's mother, Saint Anne, had also been immaculately conceived was also accepted, though not made part of Church dogma. Not all of the ideas the Church absorbed were popular beliefs—some were the beliefs of the sophisticated. It was the Platonists, so mindful of the dignity of man, who insisted that the soul was immortal. The immortality of the soul was not accepted as a dogma of the Church until the Lateran Council of 1513. The contradictory claims of mysticism and materialism were not resolved by the Church; instead, the Church embraced both and exacerbated the obvious tension betwen the warring polarities. Pictures of saints, statues, relics, rosaries, and many other of the material objects of Church ritual were crafted and manufactured in response to popular demand for miraculous images, for objects that a materialistic congregation could touch and feel.

Because the Church had so lost its moral authority, individual preachers often rose up with prophecies of fire and brimstone, the death of princes, and horrible punishments for evil monks and popes. Girolamo Savonarola enthralled Florentines at the end of the fifteenth century with his terrifying sermons. Born in Ferrara in 1452, Savonarola arrived in Florence in 1489 and commenced to foretell the deaths, plagues, invasions that were in store for unrepentant sinners.

Go thou to Rome [he preached in a harsh, high-pitched voice] and throughout Christendom; in the mansions of the great prelates and great lords there is no concern save for poetry and the oratorical art. Go thither and see, thou shalt find them all with books of the humanities in their hands. . . . O Lord, we are become the despised of all nations. . . . O Lord God . . . Thou hast cast us out from Thy presence! Hasten then the chastisement and the scourge . . . banish evil, so that the kingdom of our blessed Lord, Jesus Christ, may flourish in the world. The only hope that now remains to us, is that the sword of God may soon smite the earth.

Savonarola attacked the new learning, the new hedonism, the new materialism, and he called up a wave of anxiety to afflict all those who were uncertain about the new age they were entering. Botticelli not only became one of Savonarola's followers, the painter also repudiated his previous, pagan works and burned all of the studies of nudes that remained in his shop. Pico, Ficino, Poliziano, all came to hear, and to be disturbed by this last great voice to be raised against the rationalism, materialism, and worldliness that was taking over the lives of clergy and laymen alike. Sixty years later, Michelangelo would say that he could still hear Savonarola's shrill voice ringing in his ears.

Savonarola was by no means the only famous preacher of repentance during the Renaissance. Bernardino of Siena delved right into the details of marriage contracts and the public debt in his fiery sermons. Roberto da Lecce was known especially for preaching against violence and for attempting to patch up feuds. Others wandered about Italy denouncing the Church hierarchy and threatening divine retribution. Of them all, however, Savonarola left the most searing impression on the fifteenth century.

Savonarola had been rebuffed at the age of nineteen by a young woman, and soon after joined the Dominican order—because, he wrote to his father, of "the great misery of the world, the iniquities of men, the rapes, adulteries, larcenies, pride, idolatries, and cruel blasphemies which have brought the world so low that there is no longer anyone who does good; hence more than once a day I have sung this verse, weeping: 'Ah, flee the lands of the unfeeling, the shores of the grasping flee!' . . . I could not endure the corruption of the Italian people."

Later on, Savonarola's passionate sermons attracted the attention of Pico della Mirandola, who persuaded Lorenzo de' Medici to invite the friar to Florence and set him up in the monastery of San Marco, which the Medicis had long supported with lavish gifts. From his new pulpit, Savonarola attacked both the corruption of the Church and, to Lorenzo's surprise, of the Florentine government. When Savonarola arrived in Florence, he was thirty-seven years old, short and spare, with a great hooked nose and brilliant eyes. His habit was threadbare, and patched; his asceticism, legendary.

He preached the simplicity and purity of the early Christian Church. As time went on, and his rhetoric became more inflamed, his personal passion and rage would obscure his message; but the essential appeal, and threat, of his sermons was their call to simple justice and morality, a repudiation of getting and spending, the accumulation of things, the exploitation of the poor for the sake of luxuries for the rich. "In the early Church," Savonarola declared, "the chalices were made of wood and the prelates of gold. Today the chalices are made of gold and the prelates of wood.

"Do you imagine that the Virgin Mary went about dressed as she is depicted? I tell you she went about dressed as a poor person, simply, and so veiled that her face could hardly be seen. . . . You would do well to blot out pictures so unsuitably painted. You make the Virgin Mary look like a harlot."

As for the revival of antiquity, the attempt to reconcile pagan philosophers with the teachings of Christ, the way Ovid and Plato and other classical authors were used as texts for sermons, all that was a dangerous distraction. The way to

salvation was not through reason. "Your eyes will open if you lead a good life, and a good life depends on faith. . . . Any old woman knows more about the faith than Plato."

God would punish Italians for forsaking Him, Savonarola promised: leaders would die; plague and war would scourge the sinners; Italy would become the helpless prey of foreign invaders. Predictably enough, these calamities came to pass, and, in 1494, Charles VIII led a French army into Italy. Lorenzo's son Piero tried to deal with the French, and dealt badly. The Florentines rose up, and the Medicis were expelled from the city (and were not restored to Florence for two decades). Savonarola alone seemed able to hold the people's loyalty, and he was hastily put in charge of the government.

Government, for Savonarola, was theocracy, and he proceeded to shape Florence to what he presumed to be God's will. Luxuries and vanities were the great seducer, the terrible distraction from goodness and purity. Savonarola aroused a following of impressionable boys who cut their hair short and went from house to house — invad-

ing the very sanctuary of the Italian family — to seize lewd pictures, jewelry, pagan books, and to destroy them. Men and women were put on earth as a test for eternity; the point of life was not to live well but to die pure; anything that did not have directly to do with eternal salvation was to be smashed.

In 1497, Savonarola staged a thrilling "Burning of the Vanities." A huge funeral pyre was set up in the Piazza della Signoria. On the pyre went carnival masks, women's cosmetics, perfumes, false hair, mirrors, copies of Boccaccio and of other Italian writers, copies of the classical authors, lutes and cards and chessboards, paintings of women, both portraits and nudes, and all the other symbols and totems of the new age. A Venetian merchant who was present, Burckhardt reports, "offered the Signoria 22,000 gold florins for the objects on the pyramid; but the only answer he received was that his portrait, too, was painted, and burned along with the rest." As the pile went up in flames, the spectacle was greeted with dancing and song and trumpets and bells.

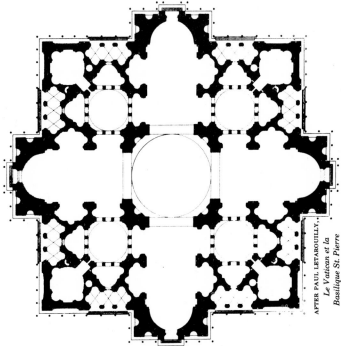

In 1503, Pope Julius II chose the plan above for a new St. Peter's Church in Rome. The work of the architect Bramante, it was based on the shape of a Greek cross, as was essential, to the Renaissance humanist mind, for any church. Years later, when it began to rise, the structure looked as it does in the drawing at left.

The "Burning of the Vanities" was Savonarola's finest moment, and his last. The Florentine oligarchs were tired of him and suspicious of his power; the Vatican perceived the genuine threat he held to all worldly institutions; the Florentines, whose homes had been so brutally invaded, hated the friar. In 1498, Savonarola was tried for heresy, condemned, and, on a platform erected on the same spot where the vanities had been burned, Savonarola was hanged and then burned, to the cheers and jeers of the crowd. He had ruled a scant four years. After his death, luxuries and vanities and worldliness revived with a vengeance.

The Medicis were restored to Florence at about the same time that one of the family, Giovanni, became Pope Leo X. As pope, Leo showed himself to be the very apotheosis of the worldly Church. His court was filled with poets and singers and entertainers, with painters and sculptors, architects and classicists. He spent all the Church had on glorifying the Vatican— and then he spent more. His grandest scheme of all was to leave a truly magnificent monument to

the Church united and triumphant, and he thought he could do no better than finish the program his predecessors had begun for the rebuilding of the basilica of St. Peter. Raphael reviewed the plans and informed Leo that it would cost one million ducats to finish the church. In order to raise the money, Leo appointed a staff of indulgence sellers to spread out through Europe, to sell indulgences for the fund for St. Peter's in Avignon, and in Bremen, Salzburg, and other parts of Germany.

With the St. Peter's indulgence, Leo X finally set off the Reformation. With that, and with an accompanying torrent of other calamities—the bankruptcy of the Vatican, the sack of Rome in 1526, the repeated, relentless foreign invasions of Italy, and finally the Church's own Counter-Reformation—the Renaissance in Italy was killed. Its ideals and its vices lived on, of course, both in Italy and the rest of Western Europe, to form the style and the substance of the modern world. But the vast and fruitful conjunction of collapse and creativity did not recur again in Western history, until, perhaps, our own time.

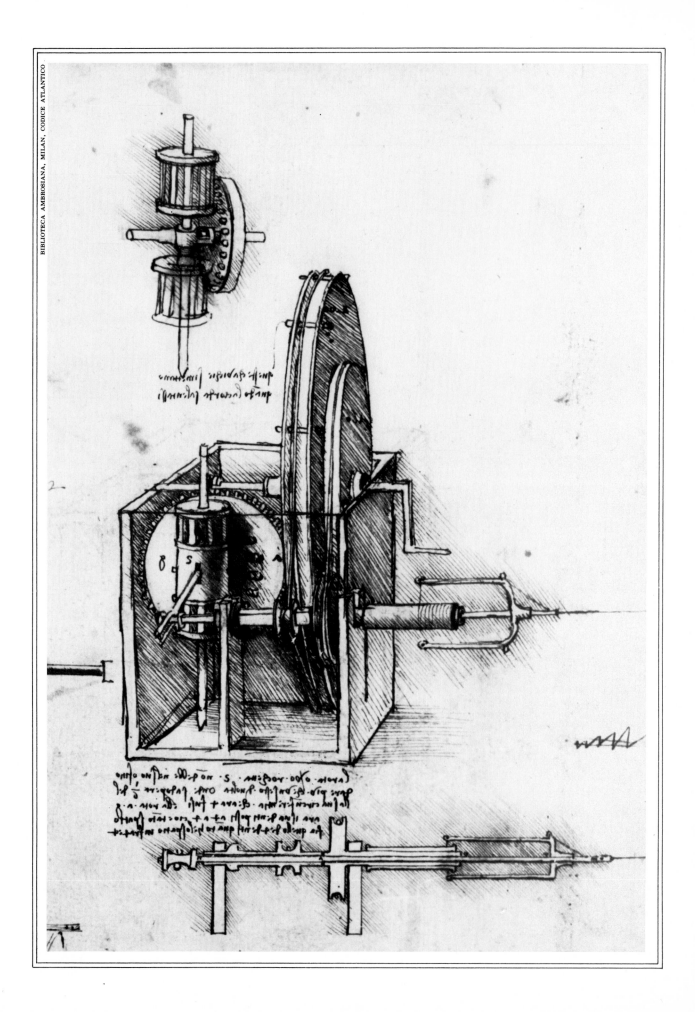

CHAPTER XI

LEONARDO DA VINCI

Leonardo was born on April 15, 1452, in Anchiano, a small village near the small town of Vinci, about twenty miles west of Florence. He was the illegitimate son of a notary, Ser Piero, whose family had been modest landowners in Vinci since the thirteenth century, and of a peasant woman named Caterina. He grew up among legitimate half brothers and half sisters (Ser Piero had

twelve children in all) in an ample, but not vast, stone farmhouse; he presumably roamed the Tuscan hills at will. Nothing more is known of his childhood; in all of his many notebooks, Leonardo never referred to his earliest years, to his family, or to any of his feelings.

Walter Pater, in his essay on Leonardo, remarked on the "lizards . . . and other strange small creatures which haunt an Italian vineyard"; such commonplaces of the country would doubtless have nourished the curiosity that a child might have about the workings of nature. Then, too, the sunlight in the neighborhood of Vinci is of an almost fierce lucidity which lends an etched vividness to the natural world. Of all his childhood daydreaming and wondering about the mysteries of nature, Leonardo gives, perhaps,

Two of Leonardo da Vinci's leading traits — ingenuity and curiosity — are demonstrated in the drawings by him on these pages. Opposite: an automatic spindle he invented. Inset above: a fetus curled up in a womb he had dissected
ROYAL LIBRARY, WINDSOR

a brief hint in his notes on painting: "You should look at certain walls stained with damp or at stones of uneven color. If you have to invent some setting you will be able to see in these the likeness of divine landscapes, adorned with mountains, ruins, rocks, woods, great plains, hills, and valleys in great variety; and then again you will see there battles and strange figures in violent action, expression of faces, and clothes, and an infinity of things. . . . In such walls the same thing happens as in the sound of bells, in whose strokes you may find every named word which you can imagine."

It was evident from his earliest years that Leonardo was uncommonly bright and talented in many areas — in mathematics, drawing, music, mechanics, in the designing and making of all sorts of objects. He was also physically beautiful, strong, and graceful. At what point his father may have noticed that he was a homosexual, and utterly godless, we do not know, but a recognition of the boy's talents, if not of his eccentricities, persuaded his father to encourage Leonardo's artistic bent. Ser Piero placed his son in Verrocchio's workshop in Florence, where the boy quickly displayed his precociousness. Of a meadow he drew, Vasari wrote that "it can truthfully be said that for diligence and faithfulness to nature nothing could be more inspired or perfect. There is a fig tree, for example, with its

117

leaves foreshortened and its branches drawn from various aspects, depicted with such loving care that the brain reels at the thought that a man could have such patience."

Leonardo's ability to capture the subtlest, most intricate details of nature was the stuff of instant legend. Vasari also reports that a peasant from Vinci asked Ser Piero to arrange to have a rude wooden shield decorated. Ser Piero gave the shield to his son, who painted on it a monster made up of parts of "lizards, crickets, serpents, butterflies, locusts, bats, and various strange creatures of this nature." When Ser Piero went to pick up the shield, he was "completely taken by surprise and gave a sudden start, not realizing

Leonardo constantly sought practical solutions to problems — with mixed results. The mechanism below, a tempered spring, would not actually have worked, since its teeth are of a constant pitch; but the mortar and the shrapnel bombs at right worked, as time would show, all too well.

that he was looking at the shield and that the form he saw was, in fact, painted on it."

The contemporaries of Leonardo were impressed by the beauty of his paintings, by the uniqueness of his compositions; but, above all, they were impressed by his apparent command of the innermost secrets of the workings of nature, and by the way he mastered light and shadow to render the world in a supremely naturalistic, and often mysteriously sinister, twilight. Of the *Mona Lisa*, Vasari wrote:

If one wanted to see how faithfully art can imitate nature, one could readily perceive it from this head; for here Leonardo subtly reproduced every living detail. The eyes had their natural lustre and moistness, and around them were the lashes and all those rosy and pearly tints that demand the greatest delicacy of execution. The eyebrows were completely natural, growing thickly in one place and lightly in another and following the pores of the skin. The nose was finely painted, with rosy and delicate nostrils as in life.

The mouth, joined to the flesh-tints of the face by the red of the lips, appeared to be living flesh rather than paint. On looking closely at the pit of her throat one could swear that the pulses were beating.

Vasari was amazed by Leonardo's paintings; he marveled at them; he admired them; but he did not much like them. In truth, Leonardo's paintings are not likable, and it appears, too, that Leonardo did not much like painting. When he died at the age of sixty-seven he had produced only about a dozen paintings. In many of them he appears to have been most interested in exploring a technical or compositional innovation, in proving or illustrating a theoretical point. His paintings often seem like more or less successful laboratory experiments. He left a good many works unfinished. He was as famous for leaving things unfinished as he was for his finished works; and he seems simply to have lost interest in the final product once he solved the prob-lem he set for himself—unless, as in the *Mona Lisa,* it was the very delicacy of the finish that intrigued him.

No piece of sculpture by Leonardo has survived, nor is it clear that he ever made more than a few small sculptures. His most ambitious project was to make, or think about making, a bronze equestrian statue of Francesco Sforza in Milan. He began work on the statue in 1491 and abandoned the idea in 1499, never having gotten further than a clay model of the horse. The model itself, however, was one of the wonders of Milan —not because it was beautiful, but because it was huge, and all who saw it were impressed by its size and puzzled over how the brilliant Leonardo was going to cast such a large piece in bronze. As it turned out, Leonardo had no idea how to cast the statue. The horse alone, without the rider, was meant to be twenty-three feet high—nearly twice the height of Verrocchio's famous Colleoni statue in Venice—and

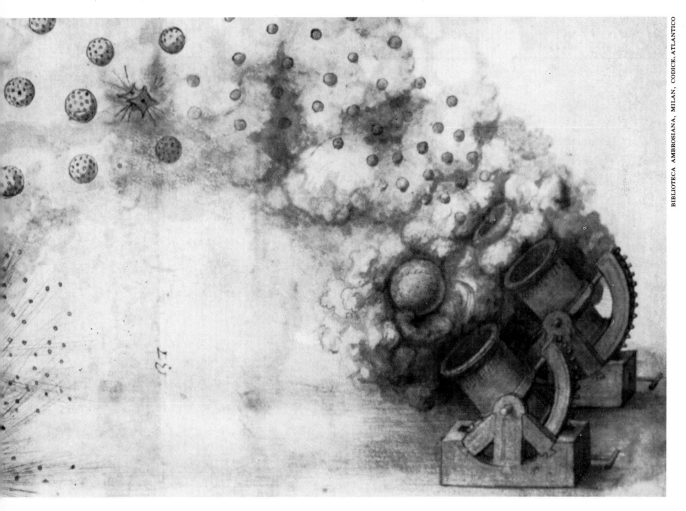

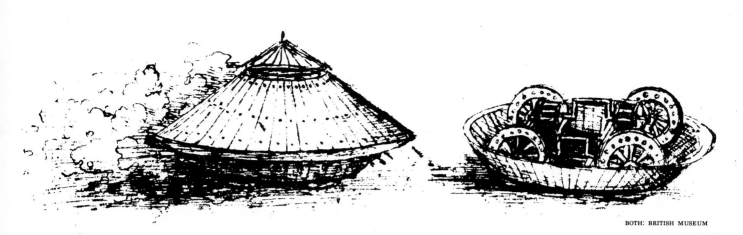

BOTH: BRITISH MUSEUM

to weigh 158,000 pounds. Leonardo evidently loved horses all his life, and made many sketches of the animals. Yet, when he came to work on his equestrian statue, his notebooks are filled as much with sketches of casting techniques as they are with sketches for the aesthetics of the design. The problem, as Leonardo defined it for himself, was one of a bravura technical performance, and he filled page after page of his notebooks with ideas for molds, bracings, casting pits, the design of ovens, winches, and other matters of techniques and materials.

To speak of Leonardo as an artist and sculptor, then, is to speak of only a small portion of the mysteries that engaged his curiosity. In his letter to Lodovico Sforza, Leonardo advertised himself as a designer of transportable bridges, military fortifications and weapons, buildings, waterworks, and other devices. Having grown up in Florence, he was inevitably interested in the textile business, and he worked out many designs of mechanisms (such as the one on page 116) for use in the textile mills. He was not content, however, with simply making workable devices; he explored the subject of mechanics down to the irreducible elements of machines. The basic elements of machines were first systematically defined at the Ecole Polytechnique in the early nineteenth century: there were thought to be twenty-two elements, including such devices as screws, bearings, axles, flywheels, ratchets. Leonardo had discovered and studied them all.

Leonardo first appeared in Milan bearing a silver lyre as a gift for Lodovico Sforza. He had an excellent singing voice, and was evidently one of the masters of his day of the lyre, a seven-stringed instrument that was both plucked and played with a bow. Once again, he was not content merely to perform, but invented new musical instruments, including mechanized drums,

drums on which melodies could be played, keyboards for wind instruments, and a device he called a *viola organista* — a keyboard instrument that activated circular bows against strings to produce a continuous tone. Nor did he stop with the invention of these novelties; he investigated the nature of acoustics; he made anatomical studies of the larynx and trachea in search of the mechanism that permitted change of pitch in the human voice; he explored the way in which sounds are made by bells, organ pipes, bellows. Music, Leonardo said, was the "shaping of the invisible," and he searched always for some way to make the invisible concrete.

His notebooks are filled, too, with attempts to master the invisible passage of time; he designed clocks and parts of clocks, to mark minutes, hours, lunar phases, and planetary positions. He was obsessed with ideas of movement, continuity and discontinuity, relationships, harmonies — abstractions that could be expressed and understood in some tangible form.

In the field of military design, his work was presumably more immediately practical. Yet, here too, it would be a mistake to assume that Leonardo was simply a utilitarian military engineer. In this eminently practical discipline, his imagination ran wild. He worked out schemes for attaching extra lances to a warrior's horse, for building fortresses with rounded walls, for diverting the entire Arno River in order to deprive Pisa of that source of water, for huge siege engines, for repeating rifles, for paddle-wheel boats, gigantic catapults, water-cooled machine guns, breach-loading cannon, matchlocks and wheel locks, directional fins for missiles. He invented a one-man battleship armed with a mortar that fired incendiary shells. Among his designs for cannon were monsters that belched great spheres that would explode on impact and scatter shrapnel. He was intrigued

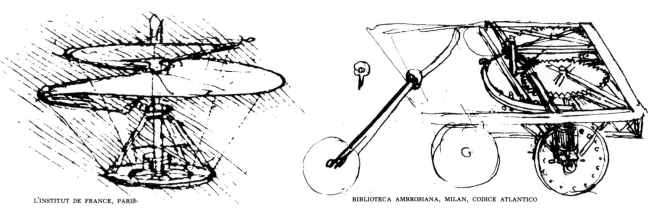

by any device that would exceed muscle power, of course; he was also particularly enamored of automatic devices, weapons that did not depend upon the control of men for their effectiveness. He liked, as Bern Dibner has written, "the constancy of the natural laws" that govern machines, "and the invariable honesty of their behavior. Unlike the men and women about him, they performed their work free of emotion, vanity, or influence."

At Milan, one of Lodovico Sforza's most urgent problems was the regulation of the Po River for purposes of irrigation. One of the sources of the Sforzas' income was the sale of water, and so Leonardo had some practical motivation to try to measure the flow of water through an irrigation canal. He sketched dams, locks, tunnels, sluice gates. He investigated water power, the force of waterfalls, and he made innumerable, and beautiful, drawings of the ways in which water flows. Leonardo's fascination with water reflected a fascination with fundamental mysteries of movement and energy that permeated both his science and his art. His drawings of flowing, bubbling, whirling water are reminiscent of his paintings, and in one of his notebooks he wrote: "Observe how the movement of the surface of the water resembles that of hair, which has two movements, one of which stems from the weight of the hair and the other from its waves and curls."

The relationships and correspondences among the elements of earth, air, water, and fire led Leonardo to look for fundamental laws of nature, laws that he probed in experiment after experiment and that always eluded him. His notebooks became a vast compendium of facts, random insights, tantalizing clues to the mysteries of nature; but he was never able to impose any order on all his observations.

He jotted down general principles of me-

Leonardo liked to "pre-imagine," as he put it, what was to be, and to make drawings of his visions. His armored tank (facing page, upright and overturned) was centuries ahead of its time in concept, but the hand-turned crank that was to move it would hardly have sufficed for the job. On this page are two inventions of his that would have worked—a helicopter, left, and a spring-propelled automobile.

chanics, or light, or sound, and added a few specifics in support of his theses—as though each general principle were to form a chapter of a book that would explain, quite simply, everything. But the chapters never take shape, generalizations lie in unsupported isolation in the notebooks; the pages are crowded with random observations that relate to nothing else, lead nowhere. Taken as a whole, the notebooks resemble nothing so much as a nightmare, lit by brilliant insights, filled with useful observations, and finally overcome by disorder and confusion and the sheer weight of unrelatable facts.

Leonardo's mind reached out to explain earth, air, water, and fire; to explain movement, force, energy, power; to understand geology and human anatomy, the flight of birds and the sounds of the human voice. In his quest for understanding, he made some splendid paintings and some designs for tanks and guns, bridges, buildings, flying machines, possibly even a bicycle. He seemed to believe that if he acquired mastery over a sufficient body of facts, if he could ever fully explain how the material world worked, he would have discovered the ultimate truth of life. Perhaps his own obsession with this quest can only be explained by his unique psychological make-up—and, one might guess, by the circumstances of his birth. Yet, whatever the personal causes for Leonardo, his belief that truth lay in the material world made him the first wholly modern man, a materialist on a heroic scale.

Despite the fact that he so often left things

121

unfinished, he was greatly sought after. Patrons sometimes lost patience with him, but they continued to support him in the hope that he would finally unlock some extraordinary secret and share it with them. His bizarre researches, his strange bits of knowledge, made him seem to his contemporaries like some mysterious, alchemical phenomenon of nature. During his career, he moved with relative ease among the courts of Italy. He spent a long time, from the age of thirty to forty-seven, in Milan (1482–99). He was employed by Cesare Borgia for a time as a military engineer, and made extraordinary aerial-view maps for Borgia. He returned to Milan in 1506, and in 1507, he entered the service of King Louis XII of France, who described Leonardo as "our regular painter and engineer." From 1514 through 1516, he tried to work for Pope Leo X in Rome, but their relationship was not ideal. Leo did not understand Leonardo's preoccupation with geometry or his little experiments of bizarre sorts. According to Vasari:

Leonardo used to get the intestines of a bullock scraped completely free of their fat, cleaned and made so fine that they could be compressed into the palm of one hand; then he would fix one end of them to a pair of bellows lying in another room, and when they were inflated they filled the room in which they were and forced anyone standing there into a corner. Thus he could expand this translucent and airy stuff to fill a large space after occupying only a little, and he compared it to genius.

Leo was not amused.

In these last years, too, Leonardo seems to have lost faith in the world he had so long investigated. In 1512, he commenced a series of studies of embryology, including a sketch—the first such sketch ever made as far as is known—of a child in a womb, which is rendered with cool, if not chilling, detachment. The last anatomical drawing he ever made, in January of 1513, was of a heart. Beginning in 1513, he also worked on his last painting, one of Saint John the Baptist. The prophet is a sinuous, fleshy, androgynous youth, with a tantalizing smile, who raises his right hand to point upward and out of the painting—as much as to say that truth lies elsewhere.

In 1514, Leonardo commenced a series of drawings called *The Deluge*. In these drawings,

the forces of nature turn on the world and destroy it. First wind and water buffet and drown the earth. Then the earth itself, in the form of a mountain, is heaved up and falls on a town. At last, as he described his own drawings, "the ruins of the high buildings in these cities will throw up a great dust, rising up in shape like smoke or wreathed clouds against the falling rain. . . .

"Ah! what dreadful noises were heard in the air rent by the fury of the thunder and the lightnings it flashed forth. . . . Ah! how many you might have seen closing their ears with their hands to shut out the tremendous sounds made in the darkened air by the raging of the winds mingling with the rain, the thunders of heaven, and the fury of the thunder-bolts."

He spent the last few years of his life at Amboise under the patronage of Francis I, no longer painting, no longer pursuing his researches with diligence, kept by the French king as one of the amazing phenomena of the world. If most of his life was characterized by sketches probing for the secrets of nature, perhaps none is more characterisitc of the end of his life than the one on the opposite page, in which a torrent of machines and tools and other man-made wonders falls on the earth and buries the world under junk. In his belief that truth lay in the material world, Leonardo was the prophet of the modern world; and in his despair with that idea, he was the prophet of twentieth-century disillusionment with the world that was born in the Renaissance.

He seemed, by the time he died in the spring of 1519, to have forgotten the beauties and daring and liberating humanism of his time, and to have sensed only that in his modern belief in materialism he had been irretrievably wrong. Or perhaps he did cling to those Renaissance discoveries that were life-enhancing, and came to realize in an ultimate leap of precociousness, as scientists and philosophers of the twentieth century have, that reality, the only reality we can know, lies in the mind, and that the mind is tragically finite. "Water struck by water," he wrote in one of his disconnected notes, "forms circles around the point of impact; the voice in the air creates the same along a greater distance; fire goes still farther, and still farther the mind in the universe; but since the universe is finite, the mind does not reach infinity."

"Oh human misery," Leonardo wrote under this drawing, "of how many things you make yourself the slave for money!"

Staff for this Book

Editor   Joseph J. Thorndike
Managing Editor   Beverley Hilowitz
Art Director   Elena M. Bloomfield
Picture Editor   Ellen F. Zeifer
Copy Editor   Kaari Ward
Assistant Editor   Sandra J. Wilmot
European Bureau   Gertrudis Feliu, *Chief*

AMERICAN HERITAGE PUBLISHING CO., INC.

President and Publisher   Paul Gottlieb
General Manager, Book Division   Kenneth W. Leish
Editorial Art Director   Murray Belsky

Acknowledgments

In the preparation of this book, the editors and author have enjoyed the help of many institutions and individuals. We would like particularly to thank the following:

Institute for Medieval and Renaissance Studies, City College, New York
 Professor Madeleine Cosman
 Daniel Furman
Scala Fine Arts Publishers, New York and Florence
Mrs. Bianca Gabbrielli, Rome
Mrs. Christine Sutherland, London
Madame Maria Todorow, Florence

Permissions

The excerpts on the pages listed below have been reprinted from the following books with the kind permission of their publishers:

Pages 5, 14: *The Portable Renaissance Reader,* James Bruce Ross and Mary Martin McLaughlin, eds. New York, Viking Press, Inc., 1958.

Pages 10, 19, 22: *Life in Italy at the Time of the Medici,* by John Gage. New York, G. P. Putnam's Sons, 1968.

Pages 10, 22, 23, 28: *The Chronicles of a Florentine Family, 1200–1470,* by Ginevra Niccolini di Camugliano. London, Jonathan Cape Ltd., 1933.

Pages 13, 42, 43, 48: *A Florentine Diary from 1450 to 1516,* by Luca Landucci, trans. Alice de Rosen Jervis. New York, E. P. Dutton & Company, 1927.

Pages 53–60, 63, 64–66: *The Book of the Courtier,* by Baldassare Castiglione, trans. Charles S. Singleton.

Garden City, N.Y., Anchor Books, Doubleday and Company, copyright © 1959 by Charles S. Singleton and Edgar de N. Mayhew.

Pages 73, 74: *Isabella d'Este,* by Julia Cartwright. Two volumes. New York, E. P. Dutton & Company, 1915.

Bibliography

General Works

Braudel, Fernand. *Capitalism and Material Life, 1400–1800.* New York, Harper & Row, 1973. Braudel is perhaps the best practitioner of the "new history," which concentrates on the details of daily life— the food, drink, drugs, fashions, clothes, houses, and technology of ordinary living.

Burckhardt, Jacob. *The Civilization of the Renaissance.* New York, Oxford University Press, 1945. Still the monument of Renaissance interpretation, for all the chipping that has been done around its base.

Burke, Peter. *Culture and Society in Renaissance Italy, 1420–1540.* New York, Charles Scribner's Sons, 1972. A quanti-

fying book—how many paintings were done of the Virgin, how many classics were published by the Aldine Press— that is dry but has many illuminating facts.

Cronin, Vincent. *The Florentine Renaissance.* London, Collins, 1967. An eminently readable popular account of the Renaissance.

Hale, J. R. *Renaissance Europe.* New York, Harper & Row, 1971.

Laven, Peter. *Renaissance Italy, 1464–1534.* London, B. T. Batsford Ltd., 1966. General background on history, politics, religion, art, architecture, and so forth.

Plumb, J. H. *The Horizon Book of the Renaissance.* New York, American Heritage, 1961.

Specialized Books

Brucker, Gene A. *Renaissance Florence.* New York, John Wiley & Sons, 1969.

Camugliano, Ginevra Niccolini di. *The Chronicles of a Florentine Family, 1200–1470.* London, Jonathan Cape Ltd., 1933.

Cartwright, Julia. *Isabella d'Este.* New York, E. P. Dutton & Company, 1915.

Chambers, D. S., ed. *Patrons and Artists in the Italian Renaissance.* London, Macmillan, 1970.

De Roover, Raymond. *The Rise and Decline of the Medici Bank, 1397–1494.* New York, W. W. Norton & Company, Inc., 1966.

Gage, John. *Life in Italy at the Time of the Medici.* New York, G. P. Putnam's Sons, 1968.

Goldthwaite, Richard A. *Private Wealth in Renaissance Florence, A Study of Four Families.* Princeton, N.J., Princeton University Press, 1968.

Hale, J. R. *Machiavelli and Renaissance Italy.* New York, Collier Books, 1960.

Mallett, Michael. *Mercenaries and Their Masters.* Totowa, N.J., Rowman & Littlefield, 1974.

Martines, Lauro. *The Social World of the Florentine Humanists, 1390–1460.* London, Routledge & Kegan Paul Ltd., 1963.

Reti, Ladislau, ed. *The Unknown Leonardo.* New York, McGraw-Hill Book Company, 1974.

Rubinstein, Nicolai, ed. *Florentine Studies, Politics and Society in Renaissance Florence.* Evanston, Illinois, Northwestern University Press, 1968.

———. *The Government of Florence Under the Medici, 1434 to 1494.* New York, Oxford University Press, 1966.

Staley, Edgcumbe. *The Guilds of Florence.* New York, Benjamin Blom, 1967.

Renaissance Writers

Bishop, Morris, ed. *A Renaissance Storybook.* Ithaca, N.Y., Cornell University Press, 1971. Short stories by Renaissance writers.

Castiglione, Baldassare. *The Book of the Courtier,* trans. Charles S. Singleton, Garden City, N.Y., Anchor Books, Doubleday and Company, 1959.

Guicciardini, Francesco. *The History of Florence.* New York, Harper Torchbooks, 1970.

Landucci, Luca. *A Florentine Diary from 1450 to 1516,* trans. Alice de Rosen Jervis, New York, E. P. Dutton & Company, 1927.

Machiavelli, Niccolò. *The Literary Works of Machiavelli,* ed. John R. Hale. London, Oxford University Press, 1961.

———. *The Prince and the Discourses.* New York, The Modern Library, 1950.

Ross, James Bruce, and Mary Martin McLaughlin, eds. *The Portable Renaissance Reader.* New York, Viking Press, Inc., 1958.

Ross, J., ed. and trans. *Lives of the Early Medici as Told in Their Correspondence.* Boston, Gorham, 1911.

Vasari, Giorgio. *Lives of the Painters,* trans. E. L. Seeley. London, Allen & Unwin, 1960.

Additional Picture Information

p. 3 Detail, *A Miracle of San Bernardino,* by Fiorenzo di Lorenzo; Pinacoteca Vannucci, Perugia. **p. 4** *Sheltering Pilgrims,* by Francesco Ubertini Bacchiacca. **p. 6** Detail, The Works of Mercy, school of Domenico Ghirlandaio; Church of Buonuomini di San Martini, Florence. **p. 11** The Works of Mercy, *Giving Linen to the Poor,* school of Domenico Ghirlandaio; Church of Buonuomini di San Martini, Florence. **pp. 12–13** *The Race of the Palio in the Streets of Florence,* by Giovanni di Francesco. **p. 14** Detail, *Founding of the Foundlings' Hospital,* by Bernardino Poccetti. **p. 17** Detail, *Birth of Saint John the Baptist,* by Domenico Ghirlandaio; Santa Maria Novella, Florence. **p. 18** Detail, wall fresco by Paolo Veronese; Villa Barbaro, Maser. **p. 19** Detail, *Last Supper;* workshop of Pietro Lorenzetti in the Lower Church of San Francesco, Assisi. **p. 20** Detail, *Banquet of Herod,* by Filippo Lippi; Duomo, Prato. **p. 21** Detail, *Stories of Santa Barbara,* by Lorenzo Lotto; Suardi Chapel, Trescore. **p. 23** From the herbal *Theatrum Sanitas.* **p. 25** *Celebrazione del matrimoni,* by Domenico Ghirlandaio; Church of Buonuomini di San Martini, Florence. **p. 28** Detail, *Sword Making,* by Bernardino Poccetti; Uffizi, Florence. **p. 29** *Dream of Saint Ursula,* from *Legend of Saint Ursula,* by Vittore Carpaccio; Accademia, Venice. **p. 30** *Arrival of Saint Ursula at Cologne,* from *Legend of Saint Ursula,* by Vittore Carpaccio; Accademia, Venice. **pp. 32–33** Drawing of the façade of the Medici bank in Milan, by Antonio Filarete; Biblioteca Nazionale, Florence. **p. 34 Top:** Wool guild emblem, possibly by Luca della Robbia; Museo dell' Opera del Duomo, Florence. **Bottom:** Caravan detail, *Virgin and Pope Callisto III,* by Sano di Pietro; Pinacoteca, Siena. **p. 35** From *Codice di Spheare,* by Marco dell' Avogaro; Biblioteca Estense, Modena. **pp. 36–37** *The Effects of Good Government,* by Ambrogio Lorenzetti; Palazzo Publico, Siena. **p. 40** Detail, *A Miracle of San Bernardino,* by Fiorenzo di Lorenzo; Pinacoteca Vannucci, Perugia. **p. 43** *The Assassination of Saint Peter Martyr,* attributed to Giovanni Bellini. **pp. 44–45** Panel, *Rout of San Romano,* by Paolo Uccello. **p. 46** Detail, *Saint George and the Princess of Trebizond,* by Pisanello. **p. 47** Detail, fresco by Piero della Francesca; Malatestiano Temple, Rimini. **p. 49** Detail, *The Triumph of Death,* attributed to Francesco Traini; Camposanto, Pisa. **p. 51** Detail, the equestrian statue by Andrea del Verrocchio; Campo SS. Giovanni e Paolo, Venice. **p. 53** Detail, *Healing of the Maimed,* by Masolino and Masaccio; Brancacci Chapel, Santa Maria del Carmine, Florence. **p. 54 Top:** Portrait of Baldassare Castiglione, by Raphael. **Bottom:** Frontispiece by Sir Thomas Hoby of a 1561 translation of Castiglione's *Courtier.* **pp. 56–57** By Giusto Van Utens; Museo Topografico, Florence. **p. 58** Detail, music fresco by Pinturicchio; Vatican, Rome. **p. 59** Detail, *The Chess Players,* by Girolamo da Cremona. **p. 60** From the manuscript *Vita B. Ioannis a Tauxignano Episcopi Ferrariae.* **p. 61** Detail, *The Journey of the Magi,* by Benozzo Gozzoli; Palazzo Medici Riccardi, Florence. **p. 62** Detail, *Birth of Saint John the Baptist,* by Domenico Ghirlandaio; Santa Maria Novella, Florence. **p. 64** Drawing of Isabella d'Este, by Leonardo da Vinci. **p. 65** Portrait of Lucrezia Borgia, by Pinturicchio; Vatican, Rome. **p. 66** From the herbal *Tacuinam Sanitatas.* **p. 67** *Lady Playing Ball,* anonymous Lombard artist; Palazzo Borromeo, Milan. **pp. 68–69** *Month of April, Triumph of Venus,* by Francesco del Cossa; Palazzo Schifanoia, Ferrara. **p. 70** *Giuoco delle palle de neve,* anonymous. **p. 71** Detail, *Month of March, Triumph of Minerva,* by Francesco del Cossa; Palazzo Schifanoia, Ferrara. **p. 73 Top:** From the manuscript *Petrus Baldus de Ubaldis.* **Bottom:** *Two Courtesans,* by Vittore Carpaccio. **p. 75** Portrait of Simonetta Vespucci, by Piero di Cosimo. **p. 76** *Saint Jerome in His Study,* presumed portrait of Cardinal Bessarion, by Vittore Carpaccio; school of San Giorgio degli Schiavoni, Venice. **p. 77** Wood inlay by Fra Giovanni da Verona; Church of Santa Maria in Organo, Verona. **p. 79** *High Table,* by Antonio Filarete. **pp. 80–81** Sixtus IV and Platina, school of Melozzo; San Spirito Hospital, Rome. **p. 82** From *Commentariorum super libro II Decretalium,* by Antonio da Budrio. **p. 83** *Ex-voto of Tommaso Inghirami.* **p. 84** Medal attributed to Tommaso Fiorentino. **p. 85** Medal attributed to Niccolò Fiorentino. **p. 86** Detail, *History of Anti-Christ,* by Luca Signorelli; Chapel of San Brizio, Orvieto Cathedral. **p. 88** by Nanni di Banco; Orsanmichele, Florence. **p. 89** *David,* by Donatello, in the Museo Nazionale, Florence. **p. 90** *The Expulsion of Adam and Eve,* by Masaccio; Brancacci Chapel, Carmine Church, Florence. **p. 91** *Last Supper,* by Leonardo da Vinci; Santa Maria delle Grazie, Milan. **p. 95** In the Uffizi, Florence. **p. 96** In the Palazzo Vecchio, Florence. **p. 97** Detail, *Nastigio-Novelle IV,* by Boccaccio; *Decameron.* **pp. 100–101** *The Adimari Wedding,* anonymous cassone panel. **p. 102** Detail, *Nastigio-Novelle IV,* by Boccaccio; *Decameron.* **p. 103** Frescoes in the Schloss Traunitz, from *Italian Actors of the Renaissance,* by Winifred Smith. **p. 104** From the Roccabianca frescoes. **p. 105** Tournament by Domenico Morone. **p. 106** Detail, fresco by Luca Signorelli; Monastery of Monte Oliveto Maggiore. **p. 107** Detail, *Fanciulli che cantano,* by Luca della Robbia; Museo dell Opera, Florence. **p. 108** Detail, *Resurrection* fresco, by Pinturicchio; Vatican, Rome. **p. 110** Detail, *Burning of Savonarola,* anonymous. **p. 111** Drawing of Leo X, attributed to Sebastiano del Piombo. **p. 112** From an Umbrian manuscript *Episodes from the Life of Franciscan Monks.* **p. 117** By Gracious Permission of Her Majesty the Queen. **p. 123** *Rain of Junk,* by Leonardo da Vinci; Windsor Castle.

FRONT COVER: *Detail of the fresco "Triumph of Venus" by Francesco Cossa. Palazzo Schifanoia, Ferrara.*

CONTENTS PAGE: *Detail of "The Miracle of San Bernardino" by Fiorenzo di Lorenzo. Pinacoteca Vannucci, Perugia; Scala.*

BIBLIOGRAPHY PAGE: *Silhouette detail of angels playing lutes from the "Nativity" by Piero della Francesca. National Gallery, London.*

Index

Numbers in boldface type refer to illustrations.